Reaching Muslims for Christ

WILLIAM J. SAAL

MOODY PRESS

CHICAGO

© 1991 by
ARAB WORLD MINISTRIES, INC.

Moody Press Edition, 1993

ISBN: 0-8024-7322-9

3 5 7 9 10 8 6 4

Printed in the United States of America

Reaching Muslims for Christ

*This book is dedicated to Muslims who earnestly
desire to know God—and to Christians who joyfully share
the grace of God with their neighbors.*

*May God bring them together according to His eternal purposes
revealed in Christ Jesus.*

I have come that they may have life, and have it to the full.
John 10:10

Peace be with you! As the Father has sent me, I am sending you.
John 20:21

CONTENTS

FOREWORD

We live in a day when God is doing wonderful things to help the church reach a lost world. He is breaking down walls and giving us access to formerly isolated peoples, and He is building bridges *and bringing formerly isolated peoples to us.*

Among these people are many Muslims who have come to Western cities to study and to work. These people for whom Christ died are our neighbors, our fellow students, our fellow workers. We can show our love to them because there are no social barriers. *Whether we admit it or not, God has made us missionaries to these people; and we shall one day give an account of what we have done with these opportunities.*

How do you go about understanding Muslims and sharing the gospel with them? This book tells you. In simple, nontechnical language, it explains what Muslims believe, what they live for, and how Christians can witness to them. *Reaching Muslims for Christ* is clear, concise, and practical. I wish every Christian would read and apply what this book teaches and that every evangelical church would establish a "Muslim witness fellowship" that would help train and encourage Christians to witness to these precious people and pray for them.

For years, I've been asking God to raise up an "apostle Paul" among the Muslims. Perhaps the Muslim friend you witness to will turn out to be the answer to that prayer.

WARREN W. WIERSBE

ACKNOWLEDGMENTS

R*eaching Muslims for Christ* grows out of a dynamic group process. It came to life many years ago as a series of papers, outlines really, published by Arab World Ministries under the title *Reaching Muslims Today.* The goal of that booklet was to provoke positive interaction with Muslims, urging Christians to present and clarify the good news in a way that would address the issues raised by Islam.

This book shares many characteristics of that earlier work. It began as a simple revision of those outlines, but it quickly became a more thorough introduction to the possibilities and pitfalls of evangelizing Muslims. Throughout, out goal has been to provide practical assistance to the man or woman attempting to give clear witness to his or her faith in Jesus Christ.

Many experienced colleagues contributed significantly to this work: a timely illustration, an embryonic thought, a moment of reflection on the rough draft. The work of a few special associates must receive personal recognition. They submitted papers and written drafts that made my work light. In particular, Steve's style and manner of thinking was infectious; he stimulated me to ponder issues I had long taken for granted. Donna helped me understand women's concerns and the importance of folk Islam. Sam's insights on world view and contextualization urge us to think clearly about core values and ideals. Tim's studies in the Gospel of Luke are worth using repeatedly. Ginger used her investigative skills to compile the resources for ministry, and Ivan made valuable suggestions at several important points. This book is largely the product of their labor. These brothers and sisters have my deepest thanks.

Co-workers in my own office helped in checking and proofreading the manuscript. Several assisted in preparing the indexes. My thanks to all of them. Special heartfelt appreciation to my secretarial assistant, Pam Snyder, for her careful typing and checking of my work, not to mention the many ways in which she guarded my schedule and telephone throughout the writing process. My closest friends, Amy, Joanna, and John, unselfishly gave their husband and father to the work of this book. Without their support, my best efforts would have been grossly inadequate.

Finally, I would like to acknowledge three colleagues who have made timely contributions to my life in Arab World Ministries. My labor in this book is the result of their investment. First, Barbara Bowers, a precious field co-worker now at home with the Lord, taught me that God's work among Muslims demands patience and perseverance. Her faithfulness will always challenge me to labor as long as God gives me breath. Second, Francis Steele, my esteemed colleague in the U.S. office, reminded me by speech and life that there is no higher purpose than obedience to God's calling. Finally, Abram Wiebe, AWM's past International Director, displayed the value of persevering prayer as the key to effective witness.

This book is more than paper and ink. It is composed of living ideas designed to challenge you to greater confidence in God's heart for Muslims. One-fifth of the world's population calls itself Muslim. These need to hear of the grace of Christ and witness His love at work in our lives. My prayer is that you will dedicate yourself to display God's compassion for Muslims and begin to befriend and love Muslims for Jesus' sake.

WILLIAM J. SAAL
2 Corinthians 4:5

INTRODUCTION

PURPOSE

Reaching Muslims for Christ. The title summarizes our purpose: to help you become an effective witness to your Muslim friends and neighbors, even if you have little knowledge of what Muslims believe or how to witness to them. Muslims must be reached with the good news. Opportunities for friendship and witness are before us. Are you prepared to take up the challenge?

Reaching Muslims for Christ is not a complete reference work covering all facets of Islam. Nor is it an authoritative guide to the most effective way to share your faith. It is a collection of outlines, observations, and useful information gleaned from men and women experienced in Muslim evangelism. This is a book about witness by people actively engaged in sharing their faith with Muslims.

First, we want to provide you with a starting point for understanding Muslims generally, and your own Muslim friend in particular. It is one thing to study idealized Qur'anic Islam, and quite another to deal with the Muslim sitting nearby. Part 1 will help you to identify basic Muslim beliefs and confusions commonly shared by Muslims about the Christian faith. Treat this book as a basic travel guide to whet your appetite for the sights, sounds, and smells of Islam and the Muslim community. But like a guide book, it is a poor substitute for the richness and diversity of a firsthand visit, so plan to spend time enjoying your new Muslim friend!

Second, we want you to become an active, thoughtful listener. Part 2 focuses on specific issues that cause the greatest difficulties for Muslims. But nothing can match the insight gained by genuine friendship and concern. Questions spoken in a relaxed moment will reveal more about your Muslim friend than any book, no matter how experienced the authors. In the midst of conversation, what Muslims believe generally is not nearly as important as what your friend believes. As you come to understand those heart issues, God can provide unique opportunities to introduce His truth.

Third, we have provided one basic approach to help you get started in sharing your faith. You can find this method outlined in Part 3. Recognize that it is *a* way to witness, not the *only* way to reach into a Muslim's heart. It is unique, however, in that it will effectively expose your friend to the Bible and allow the Holy Spirit to break down religious and cultural barriers and convict the heart. You can take this basic model and adapt it to fit your situation and personal style of witness.

In the end, all of us involved with this project hope that it will stimulate you to steadfast and loving witness. As you faithfully share the good news, pray that your friend will truly submit to God through faith in Jesus Christ.

SUGGESTIONS FOR USE

Approach the study of this handbook by asking the Holy Spirit to fill you with insight from the Word of God to complement your love and concern for Muslims.

First, because Islam is a carefully constructed religious system, you should review the foundations of your own faith. Saturate your mind with Scripture. Think carefully about the doctrines of God, Scripture, Christ, man, sin, and salvation. Purchase and read at least one of the several excellent reference works on Christian doctrine. Choose from those suggested in the Bibliography, or ask your pastor for a recommendation. In spite of Islam's apparent religious sophistication, most Muslims are confused and misinformed about what Christians believe. This book will help you begin to identify and correct the most common misconceptions.

Second, each chapter concludes with a section titled "For Reflection." These are questions to encourage application and reflection on key issues. Some of the questions are designed to bring together several facets of the material. Take the time to consider them carefully. Compare your insights and conclusions with the ideas expressed by your Muslim friend.

Third, additional insight and precision can be gained from examining the Bibliography and Notes. The Bibliography does not include all of the worthwhile books, so you will want to explore a bit on your own. Consider it a starting point to launch you out into greater understanding of Islam and Christian witness among Muslims. When you begin to explore these materials you will quickly discover other important books and magazine articles.

Fourth, some of the chapters are very elementary in content and practice; use these as a gateway to further reflection and investigation. Other chapters are more technical and theoretical, presupposing some background in work with Muslims. These chapters could be saved for later reading, after you have gained some specific experience in witness.

TECHNICAL NOTES

TRANSLITERATION OF ARABIC

Koran, Moslem, and *Mohammed* are the older anglicized equivalents of common Arabic words. The more correct transliterations are *Qur'an, Muslim,* and *Muhammed.* These latter forms will be used except in quotations, where the original forms are retained. See Appendix 1 for the complete transliteration scheme.

QUOTATIONS

Qur'anic quotations are from *The Meaning of the Glorious Koran,* commonly known as Pickthall's translation of the Qur'an. We have chosen this translation because of its wide circulation and availability.[1] If you examine other translations, you will see that several verse numbering systems are in use, so special care needs to be taken when comparing translations.

Bible quotations are normally taken from the *New International Version.*

DATES AND CALENDARS

In some instances, Westerners and Muslims use different methods for reckoning dates and events. Muslim celebrations and commemorations are established according to a lunar calendar. This Islamic calendar is indicated in the text by associating the date with the notation A.H. (after the Hijra). The Muslim calendar begins with the *Hijra,* Muhammed's journey from Mecca to Medina, which took place in approximately A.D. 622. References to the Julian, or Western, calendar are accompanied by the familiar B.C. or A.D. indicators. Since the Julian calendar is based upon solar observation, Muslim holidays cannot always be accurately predicted with a Julian date.

ILLUSTRATIONS AND LOCAL CUSTOMS

Arab World Ministries has focused on reaching Muslims in the heartland of Islam: North Africa and the Middle East. The contributors are naturally more familiar with the customs and practices of Islam in those areas, so most of the illustrations in this book are taken from that social and cultural context. Be careful in drawing generalizations from these illustrations; they may not apply to your friend from Pakistan, Indonesia, or elsewhere.

WHY WITNESS TO MUSLIMS?

1. Muslims are the object of God's love. In no way are Muslims under some special condemnation that places them beyond the reach of that love.

> For God so loved the world that he gave his one and only Son, that whoever believes in him shall not perish but have eternal life. (John 3:16)

2. The expanse and depth of Christ's love for Muslims must find its expression in us. This love is our compelling motivation in witness.

> For Christ's love compels us, because we are convinced that one died for all, and therefore all died. And he died for all, that those who live should no longer live for themselves but for him who died for them and was raised again. (2 Corinthians 5:14-15)

3. Jesus Christ commands us to proclaim the gospel to everyone and in every place. Muslim resistance to the message does not relieve us of this responsibility.

> But you will receive power when the Holy Spirit comes on you; and you will be my witnesses in Jerusalem, and in all Judea and Samaria, and to the ends of the earth. (Acts 1:8)

> For the message of the cross is foolishness to those who are perishing, but to us who are being saved it is the power of God. (1 Corinthians 1:18)

4. In Christ, God has provided everything necessary for the Muslim's salvation; apart from Him Muslims are without hope.

> I am not ashamed of the gospel, because it is the power of God for the salvation of everyone who believes: first for the Jew, then for the Gentile. (Romans 1:16)

> Salvation is found in no one else, for there is no other name under heaven given to men by which we must be saved. (Acts 4:12)

5. Islam promotes a false conception of God and of the gospel, robbing Christ of His rightful position and providing a false sense of security through self-righteousness.

> And even if our gospel is veiled, it is veiled to those who are perishing. The god of this age has blinded the minds of unbelievers, so that they cannot see the light of the gospel of the glory of Christ, who is the image of God. (2 Corinthians 4:3-4)

6. God desires to save Muslims, enter into a relationship with them, and give them eternal life.

> This is good and pleases God our Savior, who wants all men to be saved and to come to a knowledge of the truth. (1 Timothy 2:3)

7. Muslims can become a new creation through the transforming power of Christ.

> So from now on we regard no one from a worldly point of view. Though we once regarded Christ in this way, we do so no longer. Therefore, if anyone is in Christ, he is a new creation; the old has gone, the new has come! (2 Corinthians 5:16-17)

FOR REFLECTION

1. Write down the names of Muslims that you know personally. Why do they need to hear the good news? Do you really believe that your Muslim friends are under the judgment of God?
2. How can you develop opportunities to communicate the gospel to these friends?
3. Make a list of your preconceptions about Muslims. Save your list. While reading this book, periodically reexamine your thoughts. Consider sharing some of your own misunderstandings with a Muslim friend. This could encourage your friend to share his or her own misconceptions about Christianity.
4. What misconceptions do your friends have about Christianity? What do they suggest about your need for preparation?
5. Develop a prayer list that includes your Muslim friends and neighbors by name. Write down one specific request for each one that you can begin to use in intercession.

Part 1

The Challenge of Islam

CHAPTER ONE

FOUNDATIONAL ISSUES

What do you think about Islam's relationship to Christianity? Many Christians see Islam as a threat, in much the same way that Communism was cast in that role for much of the twentieth century. But this perception leads to unhelpful attitudes of fear and hostility. When Islam is viewed as a challenge, helpful attitudes can flourish: prayerful concern, a desire to become better informed, and a burning heart to reach your Muslim neighbor. The fact that so many Muslims now live in the West may be seen as God's plan to bring more and more Muslims face-to-face with Christ. It is no longer necessary to leave your own neighborhood and go abroad to find them. Muslims have become our neighbors in Toronto, Amsterdam, Los Angeles, London, New York, Paris, and Sydney. In fact, Muslims are undoubtedly to be found in your community. We are to love them, defend them, and seek their good (Exodus 22:21; 23:9; Leviticus 19:33-34).

As you begin to think constructively about approaching your Muslim neighbor, it is important to remember that a variety of issues, not all religious, may affect your friendship and the communication of the good news. Some of those problems grow out of your attitudes and experiences, whereas others come from within your Muslim friend.

MUSLIM HISTORY AND CULTURE

A great many Muslims come from places formerly colonized by the countries of Europe. Those colonial powers often abused and mistreated the local populace, considering them ignorant, unlearned people to be civilized. Consequently, your Muslim friends may be very sensitive to racist or paternalistic attitudes. They may look upon Western Christians with suspicion or hostility. Remember that these attitudes have often been aggravated by generations of fear, ignorance, illiteracy, and politics. You might consider asking your Muslim friends about their country and civilization. The Muslim world has a rich history; Muslims made significant advances in astronomy, mathematics, and medicine at a time when Europe was still in the Dark Ages.

Thought patterns differ throughout the Muslim world and often contrast sharply with Western ways of thinking. A basic knowledge of Islamic history and culture will help you to be sensitive to problem areas that may develop.

MUSLIM SOCIETY

Islamic society demands strict conformity of its members. The values of individualism and personal achievement matter little in contrast to the West; it is the thinking of the group, particularly the family, that matters most. Individual behavior is thus controlled by society, leaving little scope for independent action. So your Muslim friend may be unaccustomed to making the sort of individualistic decision associated with acceptance of the gospel. Become acquainted with family members and work through the dynamic of their relationships; doing so may prove critical to effective witness. Develop a sensitive approach to Muslim family or household evangelism, remembering that converted family units are essential to the formation and stability of the local church in Muslim society.[1]

CROSS-CULTURAL COMMUNICATION

Christians and Muslims often attach different meanings to the same words (e.g., sin, prayer, faith). Some misunderstandings about Christianity (e.g., the idea that Jesus is the physical son of God) can initially be traced to this failure in communication. Listen carefully for the ways in which your Muslim neighbor uses these terms; note the questions or responses that develop after you mention them. You must choose terms wisely and carefully define them to ensure proper understanding and avoid confusion.

OTHER CHALLENGES

Islam is not simply a religious system. It is a political, social, economic, educational, and judicial system. Islam is a religion and a world. Gently and carefully probe the scope of that world as it touches your friend. You may be surprised by what you discover. For some, secularism or materialism may exercise greater influence over their behavior than Islam. Others may retain Islam only for the social and cultural identity it provides. Others are devout in faith and practice.

Many Muslims confuse the words *Christian, European, American,* and *Catholic,* especially in those countries where the vast majority of former colonists were Roman Catholic. The confusion is not entirely surprising; citizens of Britain, Canada, and the United States frequently refer to their homelands as Christian nations. Consequently, many Muslims fail to distinguish between the Christian faith and Western culture. Their experience in Islam allows for no separation of religion and state. An indication of that understanding is seen in their initial surprise at low standards of public morality among peoples they identify as Christian.

THE PERSONAL CHALLENGE

Never forget that your Muslim friend is an individual, someone to understand and appreciate as a person. No cultural, social, or communication profile can substitute for your firsthand experience of friendship. Be prepared for many surprises along the way. Do not be afraid to ask questions and explore ideas of every sort. The goal is genuine friendship, which in turn will provide strategic opportunities for evangelism.

FOR REFLECTION

1. How would you describe the attitudes of your Christian friends toward Islam and Muslims? What factors have contributed to the development of those attitudes?
2. What specific issues have created a barrier to your Muslim friend's awareness of Christianity and the good news? How might you begin now to address those issues?
3. Begin to keep a diary of religious terms. Try to summarize your friend's understanding of key religious ideas.
4. If your Muslim friend is from a different culture, do some research about his (or her) country of origin. Ask your friend to help you understand some of the things you discover.
5. Develop three specific ideas to strengthen the relationship you enjoy with your Muslim friend.

CHAPTER TWO

UNDERSTANDING ISLAM

The word *Islam* comes from an Arabic root denoting submission. In religious usage, it is commonly understood to mean submission to God. Adherents to this religion are called Muslims (i.e., those who are submitted). The Muslim attitude toward religion is governed by Qur'an 4:125:

> Who is better in religion than he who surrendereth his purpose to Allah while doing good (to men) and followeth the tradition of Abraham, the upright? Allah (Himself) chose Abraham for friend.

Islam seeks to be a religion of submission to God; a submission that ideally manifests itself in a variety of externals, most notably in the doing of good works. Muslims believe that Abraham was a follower of Islam; as such, his life is exemplary and worthy of imitation.

In order to better understand the development of Islam as a religious system, it is necessary to examine the history of Islam. This history is particularly important when viewed against the culture of pre-Islamic Arabia.

THE RISE OF ISLAM

In Arabia, the time before Islam is known as *the period of ignorance.* The region was populated mainly by polytheistic desert nomads, some of whom believed in one supreme God surrounded by many lesser deities. Daily routine was largely governed by superstition. The city of Mecca, in western Arabia, an economic and religious center, reflected much of that superstition. At the crossroads of several trade routes, the Meccans developed their pantheon as a means to consolidate economic power. Pilgrims and trade from the surrounding tribes were drawn to a shrine, the Ka'aba, at Mecca.

Though the Bible had been translated into several languages (e.g., Coptic, Ethiopic, Syriac) before the sixth century, the New Testament was probably not translated into Arabic until A.D. 720 (i.e., about a century after the time of Muhammed). So although scattered groups of Jews and Christians lived on the Arabian Peninsula in the years prior to Islam, there seems to have been little spiritual vitality among those Christians and little effort to evangelize the pagan tribes.[1]

Muhammed was born about A.D. 570 in Mecca. It is likely that he was exposed to some Jewish and Christian teaching during his travels with trade caravans, and those influences can be noted in the development of Islam. He was religious and contemplative by nature, and after his marriage to Khadijah, a wealthy widow, he was free to devote increasing time to meditation. In a vision received in a cave at Hira, he felt himself called to be the prophet of God. He was burdened to warn the Arabs about the coming judgment day and to bring them into complete obedience and submission to the one God in order to escape His anger. At first he told only his friends of the visions; years later he shared the message with outsiders.

As one might expect, there was much opposition in Mecca because this teaching threatened the religious and economic balance of the city. So enthusiastic admirers carried the word to the nearby city of Medina. In A.D. 622, Muhammed moved to Medina to avoid persecution. This event, called the *Hijra,* is the starting point in the Islamic calendar.

Muhammed was a man of strong personality and will, a powerful administrator with the ability to make his followers feel well-respected and fairly treated. Those skills, and the loyalty of his followers, enabled the new religion to spread quickly throughout the Arabian peninsula. After Muhammed's death in A.D. 632, *caliphs* (successors to the prophet) carried Islam across North Africa, Asia, and into southern Europe. Less than a century after Muhammed's death, Islam had become a religious force encompassing the economic, cultural, and political structure of everyday life.

THE QUR'AN

Islam distinguishes itself from other world religions by its holy book, the Qur'an (i.e., recitation), which takes precedence over all other religious books. Along with the *Hadith,* or traditions, it provides binding guidance for Muslim behavior.

ORIGIN

Muslims claim that while in the cave at Hira, Muhammed heard God's voice through an angelic or spiritual intermediary, most likely the angel Gabriel. The words of the Qur'an are said to be part of a book that exists in its entirely only in heaven. Thus, Muslims often speak of the Qur'an as having descended upon the prophet Muhammed. This notion is clearly reflected by the division of the Qur'an into *suras* (i.e., series, revelations). In no sense was Muhammed's personality or understanding involved in the message of the Qur'an; it was dictated to him.

The Qur'an was not collected into book form during Muhammed's lifetime. It was first recited to his followers who, in turn, memorized or transcribed it in various scattered portions. The first caliph, Abu Bakr, instructed Zayd, Muhammed's aid, to gather and assemble (ca. A.D. 634) the text from a variety of sources. Chief among them were the portions memorized by Muhammed's closest companions. By the reign of the third caliph, Othman, there were so many different texts available that he ordered one official version of the Qur'an to be compiled and approved. In A.D. 657, all previous texts were condemned and burned.

STYLE

Muslims claim that authentic translation from Arabic into other languages is not possible (cf. Qur'an 43:2-4). Only the general meaning, lacking the perfection and power of the original, can be rendered in other languages. So for centuries, faithful Muslims, regardless of native language, have read and memorized the Qur'an in Arabic, the very *language of heaven.* Nevertheless, despite this prejudice against translation, they are now obliged to translate the Qur'an into many other languages. The titles of these translations, which often include words such as *interpretation* or *message,* convey this prejudice.

The Qur'an is divided into 114 chapters, called *suras.*[2] The suras are arranged according to length, from longest to shortest, with the exception of the first, called *The Opening.* Some scholars have noted a linkage between the first line of a sura and the last line of the preceding one. Many suras include a notation to indicate the place of revelation, whether Mecca or Medina. In earlier suras the style is more lyrical and full of feeling. Later sections tend to less fanciful prose and a stronger emphasis on ethical teaching. Earlier suras also evidence more tolerance toward Christians and Jews; later suras reflect the rejection that Muhammed and his message experienced from both Jews and Christians.

CONTENT

Qur'anic form and content were clearly affected by political realities confronting Muhammed and his followers. Exposure to Jewish and Christian sects influenced Muhammed's thinking as well. For example, the Qur'an retells, often with changes, some Jewish and Christian traditions and Bible stories. It seems likely that these were included to develop a sense of continuity with Judaism and Christianity. Muslims claim that Jews and Christians corrupted the message of the Bible. It is said that Muhammed received the inspired and final version of God's message to mankind, to correct and replace Judaism and Christianity.

The content of the Qur'an is categorized by three essential features: warnings of coming judgment, stories about the prophets, and regulations governing the Islamic community. Scattered throughout the text are bits of information about the doctrines of God, creation, the spirit world, paradise, and hell. The Qur'an is primarily a call to belief in the one God, *Allah.*

AUTHORITY

The Qur'an is considered by Muslims to be a miracle from God, eternal and uncreated, sent down from heaven. Its very existence was used by Muhammed as a proof of his apostleship (Qur'an 10:38-39). The contents are considered to be true and binding upon the conduct of the faithful. Although Christians do not recognize the divine origin of the Qur'an, it is important for you to be exposed to its content. You may struggle with the expressions, style, and thought patterns. But as you begin to share the good news with Muslims, you will discover insight into your friend's perspective. It may also prove valuable when you encourage Muslims to read the Bible.

THE HADITH

In addition to the Qur'an, Muslims rely on the *Hadith,* or tradition. The traditions form a vast library of recollections about what Muhammed (or his companions) said and did. Some of the material also comes from Jewish and Christian tradition. Since Islam seeks to answer scores of questions and legislate many details of life, these collected traditions cover all sorts of subjects: moral teaching, religious duties, legal problems, stories about the prophets and the world to come.

The authority of tradition is based on the notion that everything Muhammed said or did was revelatory. Some Muslims suggest that the Hadith has the same authority as the Qur'an, but most put it on a lower level. Basically, traditions act as a supplement to the Qur'an. Muslim preachers and writers quote freely from tradition to support their viewpoint.

An example from the traditions may be helpful. This one comes from the Forty Traditions of An-Nawawi:[3]

Hadith 34

From abu Said al-Khudri, with whom may Allah be pleased, who said:

> I heard the Apostle of Allah, upon whom be Allah's blessing and
> peace, say: "When any one of you notices anything that is disapproved
> of [by Allah], let him change it with his hand, or if that is not possible
> then with his tongue, or if that is not possible then with his heart,
> though that is the weakest [kind of] faith." Muslim relates this.

There are six great collections of Muslim tradition. The editor
of the preceding example is identified only as "Muslim." Another
editor, al-Bukhari, may be the most respected and quoted of them
all.

How reliable are the traditions? Someone has said that tradition, like nature, abhors a vacuum. Whenever there was a question or crucial issue, traditions appeared to fill the gap in
understanding. Many traditions are bogus; there is much confusion and contradiction between traditions. Serious problems confront the Muslim who wants to decide which traditions are
authentic. Yusuf Al-Qaradawi acknowledges this point:[4]

> Such a subject, moreover, compels the writer to be definitive concern-
> ing many matters about which earlier scholars have differed and con-
> temporary scholars are confused. Consequently, to prefer one opinion
> over another in matters relating to the halal and the haram in Islam
> requires patience, thoroughness in research, and intellectual exer-
> tion. . . .
>   Said Imam Malik, "The word of any person other than the Proph-
> et (peace be on him) is sometimes accepted and sometimes reject-
> ed." And Imam Shafi'i commented, "My opinion is correct with the
> possibility of its being in error. An opinion different from mine is in
> error with the possibility of its being correct."

Rules have been developed to judge legitimacy, but the rules
themselves are not very good. Many quote whatever suits their
cause. But this problem is not restricted to Islam; Judaism and
Christianity also have traditions, and many of them fail the test of
historical accuracy.

Muslim tradition also poses a problem because parts of the
Gospels sound to Muslims like their own tradition. Consequently,
they may think that Christians should regard the Gospels in the
same way that Muslims look at their own traditions.

THE DOCTRINE OF ISLAM

The Qur'an clearly identifies the fundamental doctrines and principles to which a Muslim must adhere:

> O ye who believe! Believe in Allah and His messenger and the Scripture which He hath revealed unto His messenger, and the Scripture which he hath revealed aforetime. Whoso disbelieveth in Allah and His angels and His Scriptures and His messengers and the Last Day, he verily hath wandered far astray. (Qur'an 4:136)

Many Christians focus upon the practices of Islam and fail to recognize that Muslim duty is founded upon a clear system of doctrine. Muslims believe that God revealed His message to mankind; first to Jews, later to Christians, finally and completely to Muhammed. This message governs thinking and behavior, and is frequently summed up under five or six categories of belief.

ALLAH IS THE ONE AND ONLY GOD

Islam is first and foremost the religion of God (Qur'an 5:3). Every sura in the Qur'an begins with the mention of his name and a reminder of his character. Two things ought to be noted. First, *Allah* is simply the Arabic word for God; it is used by Arabic-speaking Christians as well as by Muslims. Allah is not the Muslim God per se, though it is important to remember that the Muslim conception of God differs from that of the Bible at several major points. Second, this term, Allah, underscores the strict necessity for monotheism through the inclusion of the definite article; technically, Allah means *the* God. The doctrine of the unity and oneness of God is the most fundamental aspect of Islamic faith.

> In the name of Allah, the Beneficent, the Merciful. Say: He is Allah, the One! Allah, the eternally Besought of all! He begetteth not nor was begotten. And there is none comparable unto Him. (Qur'an 112)

God is the creator of all things. He is distinguished from his creation by certain attributes; among these are transcendence, omnipotence, sovereignty, and omniscience. These characteristics are summed up in the beautiful names of God; at least one theologian has cataloged ninety-nine names that belong uniquely to God.[5]

ANGELS

Angels are the special creation of God, completely devoted to accomplishing the divine will. Islam identifies four as archangels; Jibra'il (Gabriel, God's messenger and the angel of revelation) is best known. Every person is attended by a guardian angel and two recording angels. The former protects from dangers not decreed by God. The latter sit beside a person to gather evidence for the day of judgment: one on the left to record sins and the other on the right to record good deeds and words (Qur'an 82:10-12). Similar to angels are the *jinn,* male and female beings of great importance in folk Islam.[6]

HOLY BOOKS

Holy books are the means by which God communicated with various peoples.[7] Five books are specifically mentioned in the Qur'an; four still exist in some form: the Torah, the Psalms, the Gospel, and the Qur'an. The last is most important, by virtue of the fact that it was given last and because all other books have been altered and corrupted.[8]

HOLY APOSTLES AND PROPHETS

God's apostles bear His message. The Qur'an teaches that God sent many prophets and apostles. Twenty-five are named in the Qur'an; six have particular importance: Adam, Noah, Abraham, Moses, Jesus, and Muhammed. Although Muslims have a very high regard for Jesus, they see Muhammed as the last and most important prophet. He is the *seal of the prophets* (Qur'an 33:10); Muslims believe that Jesus prophesied of Muhammed's coming.[9]

JUDGMENT

The "last day" is the time when God will judge all men, spirits, and animals according to what they have done.[10] Known variously as the hour, the day of resurrection, and the day of judgment, its reality is denied by unbelievers (Qur'an 75:3-6). At death, the soul enters a state of unconsciousness until resurrection. Between that resurrection and the day of judgment, an undetermined period of time is imposed to prompt anxiety and suspicion in the unbeliever; people will turn to their prophets[11] for intercession. A catalog of all deeds will be opened (Qur'an 18:50); good and evil works will be placed in the scales. Every infidel who has denied God's existence and unity will be condemned; eternal punishment is reserved for those who have ascribed equals to God (e.g., Christians for ascribing deity to Jesus).[12] Muslims may suffer for a time in hell proportionate[13] to their sins, but they will eventually be delivered; Muslims hope that their good deeds will be enough to cancel out their bad deeds and admit them to paradise.[14]

DETERMINISM

Determinism is the conviction that both good and evil are predetermined by God; Muslims, therefore, submit to the events that come into their lives as their unchangeable fate, brought about by the will of God. Muslim sects hold a variety of opinions on the subject, and the dogma is not always included in a listing of beliefs.[15] However, in popular religion this conviction often dominates the Muslim's perspective on God's activity in the world.[16]

ACTS OF WORSHIP

Islam obligates all Muslims to carry out five religious duties, sometimes called the Pillars of Islam, that visibly unite Muslim society. Their fulfillment imposes a discipline on the individual and the community, giving concrete expression to the Muslim ideal of life in submission to God.

CONFESSION OF FAITH

The *Shahada* is a summary formula regularly repeated by Muslims: There is no deity but God and Muhammed is God's messenger. Islamic legal scholars agree that believing the shahada and pronouncing it before two witnesses makes the reciter a Muslim. It is a witness spoken into the ear of a newborn, recited daily throughout life, and is often heard as the last words before death. It provides the structure for the call to prayer heard from minarets around the world.

RITUAL PRAYER

Salat takes place five[17] times daily. After the body is prepared through ritual washings, the supplicant faces Mecca and follows prescribed gestures while repeating memorized ritual prayers in Arabic. Prayer may be performed anywhere as long as the required forms are maintained, but on Friday it is expected that men will gather in the local mosque for midday prayers (Qur'an 62:9-10). Women may also pray at the mosque; generally a special place is reserved for them, which is shielded from the view of male worshipers.

OBLIGATORY ALMS

The *Zakat* is a kind of tithe on various forms of property and income that is given to the poor and needy. It is compulsory (Qur'an 24:56; 57:18) and should be distinguished from voluntary alms, which are given over and above the zakat. The amount is calculated by a complex formula that levies differing rates for various possessions and income. The mode of payment, manner of collection, and distribution hierarchy have also been specified by Muslim law.

THE FAST OF RAMADAN

Fasting, *Saum,* is obligatory (Qur'an 2:183-85) during the whole month of Ramadan. Muslims are forbidden to eat, drink, use tobacco, or have sexual intercourse during the time when a white thread may be distinguished from a black one (i.e., from before sunrise until after sunset). During the night hours, these restraints are lifted (Qur'an 2:187), so people frequently stay up late to eat. After a few hours of sleep, they arise before dawn for another meal. The month ends with a great feast and exchange of gifts. All Muslims are obligated to fast, except for the sick, prepubescent children, pregnant women, some travelers, and soldiers in active combat; these are urged to fast if they can or to compensate by fasting as soon as it is physically possible. In addition to the act itself, the Qur'an places heavy emphasis upon the individual's declared intention.[18]

THE PILGRIMAGE

The sacred *Hajj*, or pilgrimage to the first House of God (Ka'aba) at Mecca, must be made at least once if it is physically and financially possible (Qur'an 3:97). Numerous rites are involved that must be performed in a specified order and at a specific time in the calendar. Women may undertake the pilgrimage if accompanied by their husbands or another protector. It is also possible to perform the pilgrimage for another; this is a good work and will be rewarded on the day of judgment.

DIVISIONS AND GROUPS WITHIN ISLAM

SHI'ISM AND SUNNISM

Islam is divided into two main branches as a result of disagreements over the qualification and selection of leadership after the death of Muhammed. Some argued that leadership was rightfully passed from Muhammed to a series of *caliphs,* or successors to the prophet. These caliphs were chosen and ruled by a consensus developed among the elders of the community. Those who hold this view are known as *Sunnis.* Others held that to be legitimate, a successor must come from the prophet's own family; the logical choice was Ali, Muhammed's son-in-law. These became known as *Shi'ites,* or partisans of Ali. Quarrels between these rival groups resulted in the assassination of Ali. Hassan, Ali's son, succeeded him; he was killed, as was his brother, Hussein, who is still greatly honored among the Shi'ites as the lord of the martyrs. With this heritage, it is not surprising that martyrs and martyrdom have been given great status in Shi'ism.

The vast majority of Muslims are Sunnis. Shi'ites are found primarily in Iran and Iraq, with a strong minority presence in Pakistan, India, Lebanon, and some of the Persian Gulf states. In matters of doctrine and obligatory practice, Sunnis and Shi'ites are the same; they differ only in certain nonobligatory practices, festivals, and traditions.

A distinctive feature of Shi'ite Islam is the role and authority of the *imam.* In Sunni Islam, he is simply the leader of Friday's community prayers. In Shi'ism, however, the imam is the divinely appointed religious, social, and political leader who assures the maintenance and triumph of true Islam. Even during periods of history devoid of a visible imamate, Shi'ites believe that the imamate has continued spiritually. Shi'ites await the appearance of the true imam, or *Mahdi,* who will reconstruct a true Islamic nation. Differences of belief regarding the identity of the Mahdi have caused several subdivisions within Shi'ism; the majority hold that the twelfth imam disappeared and will return as the anticipated Mahdi. The Ismailis, a sect within Shi'ism, identify the Mahdi with the seventh imam.

SUFISM

Technically, Sufism is not a sect of Islam but an esoteric, mystical movement within both Sunnism and Shi'ism. It emphasizes inner spirituality over external form, placing great emphasis on the soul's reaching a state of absorption into God so that it does not exist independently. Because the road to this union is long and difficult, most Sufi orders function with the help of a spiritual guide (*sheikh* or *murshid*). Each order has its own well-defined path to union with God (*tariqa*). In many cases it will involve characteristic liturgy (*dhikr*); in other cases, the emphasis is upon ethical disciplines. The liturgies may include recitations from the Qur'an, devotional prayers, music, breathing exercises, dancing, or even such exotic practices as fire walking or drug use. Sufism has become a popular form of Islam in Western countries and may suggest the thirst for spiritual reality that develops alongside Islam's ritual behavior.

AHMADIYYA SECT

The Ahmadiyya sect is considered to be heretical by Shi'ite and Sunni Islam because it considers its founder, Ghulan Ahmad, to be a prophet. A key belief involves the theory that Jesus traveled to northern India, where He died and was buried. This sect is known for its strong missionary and syncretistic emphases, its adherents frequently representing themselves to Christians as people who believe in and follow Jesus.

AFRO-AMERICAN MUSLIMS

Islam has a significant following in the Afro-American community of North America. Originally a racial movement, the majority of Afro-American Muslims now belong to the mainstream of Islam.

Early in this century, Afro-American Islam had many strands. Nobel Drew Ali and his Moorish-American Science Temple in Newark, New Jersey, sought to unite oppressed peoples under Islam. Wallace Fard, and later Elijah Muhammad, through the Lost Found Nation of Islam in the Wilderness of North America, proclaimed more of a black nationalism than traditional Islam. Elijah Muhammad's most famous disciple, Malcolm X, participated in the Hajj, where he encountered orthodox Islam. He began to reject the teachings of Elijah Muhammad and was assassinated. Malcolm X had exercised a profound influence over Warith Deen Muhammad, Elijah Muhammad's son, so after Elijah Muhammad's death, Warith Deen Muhammad led the Nation of Islam back into the mainstream of Islam. The Nation of Islam was officially disbanded and integrated into the larger Muslim community.

Splinter groups from the original Nation of Islam still exist in the United States. The most significant among them uses the name Nation of Islam and is led by Minister Louis Farrakhan. Farrakhan continues the radical racist ideology that characterized the Nation in its early years. Other prominent Muslim groups in the Afro-American community include the Hanafi movement, the Ansaru Allah, and the Islamic Party of North America.

FOR REFLECTION

1. Compare the Christian and Muslim ideas of submission to God. How does your Muslim friend see your submission to God demonstrated?

2. Do you think that events surrounding the birth of Islam have any practical effect upon the thinking of Muslims today? How might those events have colored their world view?

3. Contrast the role of Jesus and Muhammed. Years ago, Christians mistakenly referred to Muslims as Mohammedans; why was this incorrect?

4. Compare the ministry of Jesus to the function of the Qur'an in Islam. What are the key differences?

5. Spend some time reflecting on the similarities and differences in the Muslim and Christian conception of God.

6. Doctrine and practice are clearly related in Islam as they are in Christianity. Are there any significant differences in the ways that Christians and Muslims deal with doctrinal issues? What about matters of practice and behavior?

7. Ask your Muslim friend to help you understand the differences between Shi'ite and Sunni Islam. Also ask about some of the sects of Islam. What do you detect from your friend's attitude? Be prepared for questions about the various branches and denominations within Christianity.

8. Have you learned anything that may explain the growing interest in Islam among many Westerners?

CHAPTER THREE

UNDERSTANDING THE MUSLIM WORLDVIEW

Have you found it difficult to understand the way your Muslim friend looks at life? How can an intelligent person claim to believe in all the prophets and all the Scriptures, but dismiss the Bible with the unsubstantiated assertion of its corruption? In a different realm, how can the fundamentalist Muslim be so confident that a return to Islamic law will solve economic and social problems when that same law did not prevent the decline of Islam centuries ago?

THE APPROACH OF DOCTRINAL COMPARISON

Christians instinctively try to penetrate the Muslim mind-set through a comparative study of doctrine. By itself, however, doctrinal comparison cannot explain the Muslim viewpoint. Despite the similarities between Islam and Christianity, the two communities operate on very different wavelengths. Doctrinal comparison cannot help you see how or why Islam is a world-in-life view that not only makes sense, given certain presuppositions, but also has a powerful attraction to the Muslim. Above all, this approach ignores a fundamental difference between the two religions in their attitudes toward doctrine itself. Islam is law-oriented rather than theology-oriented.

Doctrine is viewed in Islam as a preamble to Islamic law, the Shariah; it is a comprehensive code governing every aspect of life, both the inner thought life and overt actions. The Confession (*Shahada*) defines *right-thinking* and the Shariah defines *right-acting*. Like the five so-called Pillars of Islam, the six Articles of Faith (i.e., belief in God, His angels, prophets, books, divine decrees, and the last day) are considered obligatory; every Muslim must confess them verbally and endorse them intellectually.

Beyond these six Articles of Faith, theologians have defined the rational bases of the faith. But since the Middle Ages there has been little original thinking comparable to what we would call theology. Creative intellectual energy has been directed into other channels, such as Qur'anic exegesis and legal theory, political science, and ideology (i.e., the integrated assertions, theories, and aims that constitute a sociopolitical program). To understand the Muslim mind, you must look beyond doctrine to its total worldview.

A LOOK AT THE MUSLIM WORLDVIEW

Practically all that has been written on the subject is from a liberal standpoint that relates the Muslim worldview to a secular view of society. Although helpful, these lack the perspective we need in order to understand and communicate the good news to our Muslim neighbor.

A KEY CONCEPT: SUBMISSION

The principal idea that integrates everything into one cohesive system is found in the word *Islam* itself. The word means "submission," whereas the term *Muslim* means "one who submits"; it defines the relationship that should exist between God and man. The corresponding verb (*aslama*) means "to make peace, surrender, or submit." It is typically used of the vanquished laying down military arms before the victor. The Islamic ideal is that every aspect of life, individual or societal, should be lived in submission to God.

This ideal is expressed in the principal synonyms for God and man in the Qur'an: *Lord* and *slave*. When Muslims perform the Ritual Prayer, they recite the first sura, addressing God as "Lord of the worlds" (1:2), and bow with faces to the ground as His slaves. This ideal is also expressed in many of the most popular names Muslims give their sons, which combine the form 'abd with *Allah* or one of the ninety-nine names of God: for example Abdur-Rahman (Slave of the Compassionate), Abdul-Aziz (Slave of the Almighty), Abdul-Haqq (Slave of the True One), Abdus-Salam (Slave of the Peaceful), and so on.

It is good to recall that the Bible also speaks of submission to God (e.g., James 4:7). Submission is part and parcel of Jesus' teaching on discipleship and the kingdom of God. The theme of serving God is also familiar. Although Muslims cannot lay exclusive claim to submission, the biblical ideas of submission and service to God differ radically from the Qur'anic concepts.

FIVE BASIC ASSUMPTIONS

Five essential ideas, quite foreign to the Christian worldview, will help to explain the Islamic understanding of submission. They are assumed in all that is said and done, without necessarily being expressed in so many words. There are many other important concepts, but these uniquely give shape to the Muslim worldview.

Absolute transcendence. Muslim writings on the doctrine of God are strikingly similar to Christian theologies. Islam's doctrine of absolute transcendence, however, has significantly influenced the divergences between Islam and Christianity. Muslims insist that God is *Wholly Other* or, in the language of the theologians, *dissimilar to contingent beings.* The Qur'an declares that "there is nothing like unto Him" (Qur'an 42:11).

Christians, of course, also hold a doctrine of transcendence, but the Muslim doctrine is more stringent. The Muslim view implies that God is *unknowable;* Christians believe that God can be known (e.g., John 1:18; 14:7; 17:6). Muslims claim to have a knowledge of God, but they mean knowledge of truth about God. They insist, against the Christian view, that God does not reveal Himself to man; He only reveals His will. There is no analogical relationship between God and man such as you find in the biblical teaching that man is created in the image of God. For your Muslim friend, God's transcendence is absolute.

Human goodness. Islam holds that people are essentially good and pure (cf. Qur'an 95:4), although unfortunately weak and forgetful (Qur'an 4:28; 20:115). In the Qur'anic account of Adam and Eve, they did not intend to disobey; they simply forgot God's command. After Adam sinned, God relented and forgave him, promised him guidance, and assured him he had nothing to fear if he followed that guidance (Qur'an 20:115-27). Islam categorically rejects the biblical doctrine of a moral fall. Muslims insist that our present separation from God is due to *God's transcendence, not a sinful human nature.* Although we do sin, this results from ethical misperception and not sinfulness. We have the moral power not to sin; we do not need salvation, we need guidance. With divine guidance, we are able to live a life of submission that pleases God.

For the Muslim, our present situation is the *normal* human condition. According to the Bible, it is abnormal. God did not create us as we now are, nor does He intend that we stay in this condition. In Christ, we have the hope of being liberated from the creation's present bondage to decay and experiencing the redemption of our bodies (Romans 8:21-23). Islamic eschatology does not offer any hope of freedom from sin.

Divine guidance. A third assumption is that God has provided guidance. This is one of the central themes of the Qur'an. Guidance was found in the books of Moses and of Jesus (e.g., Qur'an 3:3), but above all in the Qur'an, which is frequently called "a guidance and a mercy for believers" (Qur'an 27:77). The Qur'an, together with the Traditions (Hadith) and certain other sources, constitute religious law (the Shariah), which Muslims believe to be the very "Law of God."

The biblical teaching about religious law is quite the opposite. Romans 8:3 suggests that religious law (in this case, the Mosaic law) is powerless to help us live in true submission to God because it is weakened by the sinful nature. For the sake of argument, you might acknowledge that the Shariah is basically good. Some of its provisions are unjust, but much of it is worthwhile and good, reflecting the general moral law of God (e.g., it forbids kill-ing, stealing, adultery, and so on). The point of Romans 8, however, is that even if the Shariah, like the Torah of Moses, were the very law of God, it would still be powerless to effect true submission to God. Reliance on law to produce submission assumes, gratuitously, that humanity is constitutionally good. On the contrary, human nature is hostile to God (Romans 8:7-8). Islam fails to recognize that the problem is with the human nature.

A Community of Submission. The preceding assumptions lead naturally to a fourth, the idea of community. By A.D. 622, Muhammed's preaching had aroused violent opposition in the city of Mecca; his life and the lives of his followers were in jeopardy. He had, however, a sizable following in the city of Medina, some three hundred miles to the north. The Muslims of Medina invited Muhammed to mediate their differences with various tribal groups in the city. So Muhammed accepted their offer and moved with his followers to Medina. That well-known event, the *Hijra,* gave Muhammed opportunity to gain control of Medina and eventually extend that control to the entire Arabian Peninsula and beyond.

This event is the pivotal event of Islamic history and has become the starting point of the Muslim calendar. Muslims believe that God's ultimate objective was the creation of a new universal social order. The Hijra marks the beginning of this new world order, today identified with the Nation or Community of Islam, the *Ummah.* Muslims consider it to be the first nation or community in history to live in true submission to the law of God. Hence, the religion of that community is called *Al-Islam (The* Submission). Muhammed himself, the supreme lawgiver, was its first head of state. He was succeeded by a sequence of *caliphs* (i.e., one who comes after) who were chosen to rule the community in his place.

That first community at Medina serves as the model community, the exemplar Muslims must strive to emulate. It is said to be superior to other types of social organization (e.g., capitalism, communism, or socialism) since it is based on the very law of God, and not on man-made law codes derived from custom and human legal reasoning. The model requires a Muslim governmental apparatus that provides the legal and social conditions necessary to facilitate observance and enforcement of the law. The hope is that a much higher degree of piety and submission to God will develop in the community than in other social systems. Indeed, Muslim government is necessary for there to be true submission. There is no separation between the sacred and the secular, between church and state. This Community of Submission is one, universal, and cohesive; it represents the kingdom of God on earth.

A heavenly culture. One further aspect of this community should be mentioned: Islamic religious culture is of heavenly or divine origin. This appears to derive mainly from the Muslim view of revelation. The Qur'an commonly describes its disclosure to Muhammed as a *sending down* of material from an archetypal scripture in heaven called the "Preserved Tablet" or "Mother of Books." Muslims draw two conclusions that lead to the assumption that Islam is a heavenly culture: the Qur'an has an absolutely unique divine status that makes it suprahistorical, and the very language in which it was revealed, Arabic, comes from God. Arabs commonly refer to the Qur'an as *tanzil* (a sending down) and *kitab samawi* (heavenly scripture), and to Arabic as *lugat as-sama'* (the language of heaven).

Several rules and practices illustrate this. First is the notion that the Qur'an cannot be translated, that many of its words have too rich a meaning to be put into any other language. Muslims believe that full understanding of the Qur'an only comes by reading it in the sacred Arabic. Second is the requirement that ritual prayers and other obligatory liturgical acts must be recited in Arabic. Third, converts are encouraged to take Islamic (i.e., Arabic) names, and Muslim parents give Muslim names to their children. Finally, Muslims are extremely hostile toward the historical-critical study of the Qur'an and Islamic history. To this day, no Muslim has ever dared undertake a textual-critical study or established a critical edition of the Qur'an. That would be incompatible with the supposed suprahistorical nature of Islamic culture, and considered tantamount to *kufr* (infidelity).

The antithesis between the Muslim and Christian worldviews is clear. From the biblical perspective, no culture, language, or community can claim any special divine status that puts it beyond investigation or makes it the standard by which everyone and everything is judged. Such a claim would stand in sharp conflict with the Christian doctrine of sin, dishonoring God while exalting and glorifying humankind.

DEEPENING OUR UNDERSTANDING OF THE MUSLIM WORLDVIEW

Certain historical factors add important nuances to the Muslim vision of community and help explain why Muslims are captivated by this worldview. They provide a broad context for understanding the development and implementation of the preceding assumptions.

Consider the long and brilliant history of Islamic civilization. By the tenth century it had become the center of world civilization, during a time when many Europeans were still uncivilized barbarians. Islamic civilization has demonstrated a remarkable resilience and ability to absorb a wide variety of peoples and cultures. In the minds of most Muslims, these facts confirm that Islam is superior to other types of societies.

As Islamic civilization matured and spread, however, a gap appeared between the ideal Islam and the real. For example, only the first four caliphs are considered to be rightly-guided (the *khulafa' rashidun*). From about the fifteenth century, Islam went into decline. Muslims experienced setbacks and loss of territory as the vast Muslim empire began to disintegrate. In the nineteenth and early twentieth centuries, the Community experienced its darkest hour. It was politically fragmented, economically underdeveloped, and largely under the control of Western Colonial powers. After the abolition of the caliphate in A.D. 1924, there was no longer a Prophet's Successor to rule the Community, as required by Muslim ideology.

You can readily understand the crisis of faith precipitated by this decline. In the Qur'an, God had seemed to promise political power if Muslims lived in submission to His law (Qur'an 63:8; cf. 24:55). There should exist, as in the days of Muhammed, a united Community in full political control of its own destiny and a center of world power. How was it, then, that they were now backward, hopelessly fragmented, and in subjection to non-Muslim powers? It was particularly galling to be ruled by infidels.

The situation provoked considerable discussion among Muslims. Most agreed that the fault did not lie with Islam itself but with the Community. Some concluded that the Community had deviated from the straight path of submission and that God had forsaken them. Others maintained that the problem was an antiquated perception of reality; Muslims had maintained a medieval understanding of the world and had ceased to keep pace with modern civilization. These differences in analysis naturally led to a variety of solutions; most attempted to reform Islam in one way or another, but a few abandoned Islamic law entirely.

CURRENT REALITIES

The Muslim world experienced a radical change in the middle of the twentieth century. In the decade following World War II, most became politically independent. Many adopted forms of government with some reference to Islamic law while being patterned on Western political models, especially socialism. Expectations were high for an economic recovery. Most of the constitutions declared Islam to be the state religion but limited the role of the Shariah as a source of legislation. A few declared the Shariah to be the sole law and authority. Most also adopted the Western concept of nationality, defining the nation in terms of citizenship rather than of religion. Secularism has likewise made inroads. The hope was that ultimately better things would result.

Now, a generation later, many are disillusioned by the grand experiment with Western models. Many believe that though their countries have gained independence, they are still not respected by the West. There is a rising tide of anger directed against their own governments, which have betrayed them. Islamic fundamentalists declare that God is against these nations because they have followed Western values rather than Islam. Pressure is mounting for a return to Islam and Islamic law. There is an increased tendency to blame the West for problems. Many see a great conspiracy against Islam in Western political maneuverings concerning Middle East regional affairs. Western decadence provides a further reason to reject Western political models.

On the other hand, economic fortunes have experienced a marked improvement. Muslims control most of the world's oil reserves. These oil-producing nations exercise considerable political and economic clout, which they often use for the benefit of Islam. There is rapid demographic growth in the Muslim World, doubling every twenty-four to thirty years. Finally, Muslims have experienced success in taking Islam to the West, especially Europe and North America. You can understand that many are confident of change and believe that once again a united Muslim community will be the dominant force in the world.

FOR REFLECTION

1. Why is an understanding of the Muslim worldview important to effective communication of the gospel?
2. Christians also believe that man must submit to God. Compare that idea of submission to what you know of Islam. How can you demonstrate your submission to God in a way that your Muslim friend can understand?
3. How will your understanding of the "five basic assumptions" influence your communication of the gospel? What problem areas can you anticipate in proclaiming the good news?
4. At some levels, the idea of a Muslim community is very appealing. Why? How does that idea compare with the biblical ideal of the church?

CHAPTER FOUR

FOLK ISLAM

THE SIGNIFICANCE OF FOLK ISLAM

The men returned from the cemetery with a word of comfort for the widow. Naturally, they had followed the usual Islamic practices at the time of burial. But there was special consolation because the grave was large enough to include the body of a stillborn baby, brought by its father at that very moment. The men had carefully inquired if the baby had cried at birth. It had not. So the head of their family (a family that includes teachers, doctors, and government personnel) was accompanied into the afterlife by an angel.

Folk Islam is a mixture of pristine Islam with the ancient religious traditions and practices of ordinary people. It exists in a world populated by angels, demons, jinn, magicians, fortune-tellers, healers, and saints (both living and dead). Every aspect of daily life, from birth to death, is governed by the spiritual realities of this world. Ordinary Muslims regularly turn to the practice of folk religion to meet felt needs while considering themselves to be genuine followers of Islam.

Any effort you make to share the gospel must regard the beliefs and practices of folk Islam. These beliefs permeate the daily routine with a binding force that Western systems of education and reason do not destroy. An intellectual denial of such super-

51

natural power does not remove the hold it has over people who recognize and fear its existence. Women, in particular, may adhere strongly to the practices of folk Islam as a way of controlling their world. They pass on those beliefs to their children, insuring continued folk practice among future generations.

RELIGIOUS PRACTICES

Folk practices and beliefs are often entwined with Islam's obligatory duties. For example, at the time of the pilgrimage, the Black Stone in the Ka'aba is venerated; pilgrims press against the area between the stone and the door in the side of the Ka'aba. They hug the curtain and call upon God. They throw stones at a pillar that symbolizes demonic power. They take water from a sacred well to anoint the sick or dying. Every prayer ritual is concluded by greeting the recording angel on each shoulder.

The concept of spirit possession finds support in the Hadith and traditional Qur'anic commentaries. Women who fear evil influence over their young children will consult specialists in magic and spiritual medicine. They may attach charms to their children in order to protect them against the evil eye of envy. Spirit possession itself is evident in the *zar* ceremonies of Egypt or in dance sessions of North Africa.

Religious brotherhoods, associated with living or dead holy men, are often heavily involved with folk religious practice. They may encourage the search for spiritual strength by chanting the names of God or venerating Muhammed. In North Africa, the landscape is dotted with the tombs of dead saints, a unique component in folk Islam. People who wish some special blessing will visit these tombs and follow a prescribed ritual that may include animal sacrifice. The *marabout* (living or dead holy person) serves as an intermediary with the supernatural and communicates God's *baraka* (blessing or grace) to his devotees. In Morocco, an annual festival or pilgrimage to one of these holy places is known as a *moussem.*

Similar practices are found in the ancient customs of these lands. Pre-Christian North Africans feared the evil eye and used charms in the form of a hand or fish to protect themselves. They honored the graves of ancestors, poured out libations on their tombs, slept nearby to receive significant dreams, and celebrated special feasts on tables near the tombs. They were preoccupied with magic and the activities of jinn and spirits. Water sources, trees, rocks, and mountains are tied in with belief of the sacred.

SOCIAL CUSTOMS

Human desires for fruitfulness, happiness, health, and success motivate Muslims to try to influence their destiny. For example, a village woman decides to practice family planning, so the henna from her wedding ceremony is carefully hidden on a plate by her mother. Later, when she wants a child, she takes her husband to her mother's home for a meal served on that special plate; soon afterward she becomes pregnant.

When modern medicine fails to cure illness, the family falls back on other powers. For example, a young woman is crippled. After taking her to doctors, the family prepares to make a pilgrimage to a local saint's tomb. She wakes up early for the journey and is suddenly able to walk. The family is convinced that she has been healed by the power of the saint's name.

A young bride finds that her husband has left her. She goes to a local sorceress and learns that the woman was asked to practice magic against her by someone in the husband's family. The sorceress decides that she prefers the bride, so she gives her a potion; subsequently the husband returns and remains faithful to her. Another young woman becomes jealous of her cousin's new bride. She had not wanted to marry the cousin before, but now she desires him. So she practices magic. He divorces his wife in order to marry the cousin.

An old man knows that he is dying, so he requests that the Qur'an be chanted by his bedside each night; he is careful to fall asleep facing Mecca. His grandson, a young student, does not want to be alone with his grandfather when death comes. He is afraid that he will not know how to prepare him in the right position to enter the afterlife.

SPIRITUAL WARFARE

Although some folk practices appear to be only superstitions, others are obviously tied in with satanic power. They hold people in fear and bondage, manifesting subservience to the Evil One.[1]

Leaders of the early church were aware of the connections between folk religion and spiritual conflict. At baptism, the new believer was asked to renounce the devil and all his works. The new catechumen was thus reminded of Christ's real victory over the kingdom of darkness. The unsatisfactory spiritual progress of some Muslim converts may suggest that they have not completely addressed the force of folk Islam in their past. Western Christians have sometimes assumed that intellectual explanations of the Word were sufficient to break long-nurtured ties to sorcery, saints' tombs, or spirit possession. A fuller understanding of folk religion emphasizes the need for a renunciation of these practices and a disciplined walk in the Scriptures under the Holy Spirit's guidance.

The Christian who ministers to Muslims must have a solid biblical foundation in spiritual warfare. The Lord Jesus strategically defeated Satan by His perfect life and substitutionary death. It is not surprising to discover that one of Satan's aims is to blind many minds to the glorious truths of our Lord's incarnation, suffering, death, resurrection, and ascension (2 Corinthians 4:4; Ephesians 1:19-23; Hebrews 2:5-9, 14-15; 1 John 3:8).

Keep in mind the following principles as you develop a biblical approach to spiritual warfare and folk Islam:

- The most significant power encounter occurs when the repentant and believing sinner is rescued from the kingdom of darkness and placed into the kingdom of God's Son (Colossians 1:13; see also Romans 1:16-17; 1 Corinthians 1:18).
- A confrontational experience with evil powers alone will not guarantee complete freedom. The afflicted individual must be born again and discipled in the faith. The discipling process is essential! Furthermore, care must be taken to address moral, physical, and psychological issues that

remain from past demonic or folk religious associations (Matthew 12:43-45; John 8:32; Ephesians 4:22–5:2; Colossians 3:5-17).

- Folk Islam shares much in common with traditional occultism; it is essentially animism with an Islamic veneer. Although much has been written on the subject of occult practices and deliverance, you would do well to carefully read a few of the best.[2]
- Any Christian witnessing to people engaged in folk religion must maintain a stable, Spirit-filled walk. Remember that authority over the powers of darkness flows from the objective work of the Lord Jesus for every believer: His finished work on the cross and our union with Him (Romans 6:1-14; Galatians 6:14; Ephesians 2:5-6; Colossians 2:15).

FOR REFLECTION

1. What ideas and practices can you find in the writings of Islam to support the supernatural worldview of ordinary Muslims (e.g., belief in angels, demons, jinn, and so on)?
2. To what degree are the beliefs and practices of folk Islam only superstitions? How does occultic power enter into those practices?
3. How do the beliefs and practices of folk Islam conflict with determinism (the view that Muslims submit to the events in their lives as their unchangeable fate, brought about by God's will)?
4. How can you apply your understanding of folk Islam and the felt needs of people to your communication of the gospel?
5. What biblical truths are essential for engaging in spiritual warfare with the forces behind folk religion?

CHAPTER FIVE

WOMEN
IN ISLAM

SIGNIFICANCE IN SOCIETY

Are Muslim women the poor-spirited, downtrodden, weak creatures sometimes presented in the media as an example of the effects of Islamic belief? Or are they the dark-eyed, exotic beauties who exist for the satisfaction of man's desires? Neither extreme accurately conveys the truth.

The status of Muslim women varies widely. Some are unjustly treated and despised, whereas others are admired and protected for their beauty. But the majority do not feebly succumb to male domination. The inner strength and power of the Muslim woman may be concealed, but it is there. It can be seen in her ability to adapt to social structures. Since family is so important in Muslim society, women exert significant influence and control. In their eagerness to keep cultural traditions, they direct the family in religious and social practices.

RELIGIOUS BELIEFS

The majority of Muslim women feel that they are spiritually equal to men. Their relationship to God follows the same rules. They pronounce the confession, pray daily, keep the fast, give alms, and go on the pilgrimage. The fact that their physical nature makes them unclean for prayer and fasting for a few days is accepted as a part of their sex-role. Some go to the mosque, entering discreetly to pray in the women's section, speaking softly so that their voices are not heard above those of men. At momentous occasions, such as birth, circumcision, marriage, and death, they may have special responsibilities governed by local custom. For example, women sit in the home and read the Qur'an all night with the body of a dead loved one; but men escort the body to the cemetery and recite the Qur'an by the grave.

Apparent inequalities between men and women are seen in terms of differing roles in society. Many explain the Qur'anic verses that give greater inheritance to male offspring on the basis that men need extra wealth to adequately care for their dependents. Religious laws governing divorce, polygamy, and child care cause distress to many women. For example, consider the attitudes that stand behind these hadiths:[1]

1. Many men have reached perfection. But of all women only four have done so. . . .
2. One marries a woman for one of four reasons: her wealth, her quality, her beauty, her religion. Get those who have religion, and you get your hands full.
3. I leave behind me no temptation more harmful to men than women.

Some modern governments have reinterpreted and modified those laws or encouraged practices that provide greater protection for women. The women themselves are not passive; with limited access to the outside world, they turn to folk religious practice and its provision of supernatural power.

CHANGING WORLD

Formal education has brought about major changes in many Muslim countries. Even in those countries where the majority of women stay at home, educated mothers are portrayed as more helpful to their children. Where economic conditions require a larger work force, traditions are adapted or discarded so that women can work outside the home. Unfortunately for those who

would like to find jobs, opportunities are limited in societies overwhelmed by large numbers of unemployed men.

The introduction of television has changed awareness of the
outside world. Illiterate women may not learn to read, but they
will be indirectly influenced by news bulletins, children's pro-
grams, and soap operas, as well as by government-sponsored pro-
grams. Teaching about hygiene, safety, and nutrition is gradually
affecting women's lives and that of their families.

WOMEN IN THE PUBLIC SPHERE

An increasing number of young women are educated and
trained to work outside the home. They carry responsibility as
teachers, secretaries, bank clerks, nurses, laboratory assistants,
salespersons, and policewomen. The less-educated may be em-
ployed as factory workers, cleaning women, or farm laborers. A
system of institutions run entirely by women has been developed
in Saudi Arabia, where there is an aversion to women working
with men. This particularly favors the advancement of women in
leadership positions.

Educated women become involved in various government
and nongovernment organizations. A few exceptional women have
received governmental leadership positions within their expertise
(e.g., engineering, medicine, education, law). These women are
concerned not only with women's interests but also with improv-
ing the economic and political situations of their countries. They
realize that efforts to improve women's rights to work are futile if
the economy of the country cannot sustain increased employment.

Although society accepts women working outside the home
when there is an economic need, it resists their unrestricted
movement in public. Such freedom goes against society's concern
for a woman's honor and that of her family. Many believe that
uncontrolled mixing of the sexes would result in a decline in public morals and social order. By wearing the *Hijab* (Islamic head
covering) or other traditional veiling, women declare that they are
religious, moral, serious women with no desire to draw men's
sexual attention. Not all women agree that such a covering is necessary to earn respect; some are disturbed by Islamic fundamen-

talist movements that incite young men to malign unveiled women in the streets.

FAMILY AND SOCIETY

The family is key to understanding Muslim society and the role of women. The family name must not be stained by any doubt about the virginity of its daughters or the paternity of its children. Normally, a young woman is so protected by her family that her movements outside the home will be restricted. Even if she attends a university or takes outside employment, she will follow family views on acceptable dress and conduct. Time outside her home will be limited to school or work; often her brothers will be close by to escort her home. If she is divorced, she will return to her father's home to wait the three months prescribed in the Qur'an before remarriage. In this way, if she were pregnant, the father of her child would be known. Under Islamic law there is no adoption, though a child may be raised by guardians.

A woman's sense of identity is tied to her family relationships. Although this has many advantages, it is often the source of great stress. As a little girl she is known as the daughter of a certain person (e.g., *bint el Hassan,* "daughter of Hassan"). Shame is used to insure behavior that will please and honor her family. When she marries, she keeps the idea of that family relationship while adding on the relationship of wife. In many societies, she will be known as the mother of her eldest son (e.g., *umm Ahmed,* "mother of Ahmed"). So she sees herself as a member of her honored family. She will not easily make decisions that incur their displeasure or the condemnation of society. Later, as a mother herself, she will develop deep emotional ties to her children. She will be the source of affection for the children, whereas the father represents discipline and punishment. She may intercede for her children before the stern male figure, or even conceal from her husband the various errors and difficulties of her children (for which she may well be blamed). In fact, these deep affective ties will continue over the years to bind her children to her, particularly her sons. These ties may, at times, cause disharmony in her sons' marriages.

The role of the older woman is a powerful one, particularly when younger women live under her direction in the extended family. For household harmony, young people may choose a marriage partner from among their cousins. Such a choice unites the family economically and insures agreement in family customs and traditions. In recent years nuclear family units have appeared as young couples move away from parents in response to job situations. This change has affected the mother-in-law's power. Even so, many grown children return regularly to the family home to spend time with their parents.[2]

CULTURAL VALUES

Key family events are important to women, with each occasion marked by careful observance of local and religious customs. For example, the Islamic confession is whispered into the ear of a newborn, and the mother is given special food. Everything is done to protect the child from the evil eye. When a wedding occurs, the celebration includes readings from the Qur'an to bring blessing; often there are local customs to recognize the bride's virginity or to ensure the birth of children. Women serve as guardians of these traditions, carefully fulfilling each obligation.

Celebrations from the Islamic calendar are remembered by special ceremonies to mark the prophet Muhammed's birthday or the feast days at the end of the month of Ramadan. Most women strictly keep the fast during that month; then they particularly enjoy the opportunity to visit friends and family in the evening or to shop for new clothing for their children. Their culinary skill is evident in the special cakes and meals prepared throughout the month.

CONCLUSION

Traditions of family and society are guarded and followed closely by women. As the home and family are important to the whole society, the women who influence and control that home life may find their personal value, identity, and role as the guardians of those customs.

Education and employment have brought significant advantages to women. But along with these advantages come clashes with deeply rooted ideals. Islamic fundamentalism calls for a renewal of orthodox Muslim values, and with it a reversion to the traditional role of women. Many younger women struggle with family expectations, including pressure to marry, arranged marriages, and dowry prices. Muslim women stand today at the crossroads of change; unfortunately for some, change exacts a heavy toll.

FOR REFLECTION

1. What similarities and differences do you find in the presentation of women in the Qur'an and in the Bible? What roles are given to women within their religious fellowship groups and within society as a whole?
2. Choose a Muslim country and investigate the lives of its women citizens in terms of laws, educational and employment opportunities, and religious customs.
3. What are the felt needs of Muslim women and how does the gospel of Jesus Christ meet those needs?
4. How would you communicate the gospel to a Muslim woman you know? What are the major hindrances to her acceptance of the gospel? How might you try to overcome those difficulties?

CHAPTER SIX

ISLAM AND CHRISTIANITY

Shortly after you begin to discuss spiritual things with your Muslim friends, you will discover several commonly held misconceptions of the Christian faith. Some are the result of specific Qur'anic allegations; others seem to be more closely related to the history of contacts between the Christian and Muslim communities. This chapter distinguishes between misunderstandings or confusion and disagreement. It catalogs the major points of confusion and conflict. Strategies for answering may be found in Part 2 of this book, "The Christian Answer."

MUSLIM CONFUSION ABOUT CHRISTIANITY

Muslims are greatly misinformed about Christian belief. They may have knowledge of certain Christian doctrines, but you must not assume that knowledge to be fully accurate or complete. Listen carefully and seek to identify basic assumptions and confusion. Patiently explain the matters that are misunderstood. Remember that lifelong confusion is not corrected easily. As the fog of confusion clears, the critical points of disagreement will be evident.

CHRISTIANS ARE POLYTHEISTS

Most Muslims are convinced that Christians worship three gods. They commonly believe that the Christian Trinity consists of God the Father, the virgin Mary, and Jesus. Muslims suppose that Christians understand Jesus to be the son of God in a human, physical sense. It is not unusual for Muslims to accuse Christians of believing that God had a wife, Mary, and that Jesus was born as a result of their physical union. The source of this confusion is the Qur'an itself:

> Verily Christ Jesus the son of Mary is the apostle of God, and his Word, which he conveyed into Mary, and a spirit proceeding from him. Believe therefore in God, and his apostles, and say not, there are three Gods. (Qur'an 4:171)

> They are surely infidels, who say, Verily God is Christ the son of Mary. . . . They are certainly infidels, who say, God is the third of three; for there is no God besides one God. (Qur'an 5:72-73)

> And when God shall say unto Jesus, at the last day, O Jesus, son of Mary, hast thou said unto men, Take me and my mother for two gods, beside God? He shall answer, Praise be unto thee! it is not for me to say that which I ought not. (Qur'an 5:116)

> Say, God is one God, the eternal God: he begetteth not, neither is he begotten and there is not anyone like unto him. (Qur'an 112:1-4)

> He is the maker of heaven and earth: how should he have issue, since he hath no consort? (Qur'an 6:102)

It is not surprising that these passages are regularly quoted by Muslim apologists. But these texts have also profoundly influenced the thinking of common Muslims.

> I have a question which torments me much: Why do you say that Jesus Christ is the Son of God when we Algerians read in the Qur'an that God was not born, and He had no children? If He had a son, this infers that He had a wife. For us, Jesus is the son of his mother, Mary, and not of God.[1]

JESUS WAS HUMAN, NOT DIVINE

Muslims believe that Jesus, as all other children of Adam, had only a human nature. In no sense did He possess the nature of God. He was a great prophet, but He was only a creature of God like any other.

> Christ the son of Mary is no more than an apostle; other apostles have preceded him; and his mother was a woman of veracity: they both ate food. (Qur'an 5:75)

> Verily the likeness of Jesus in the sight of God is as the likeness of Adam: he created him out of the dust, and then said unto him, 'Be'; and he was. (Qur'an 3:59)

The human qualities of Jesus necessarily clash with the Muslim conception of God. The Muslim reasons: God is so different from us—how could He engage in such physical activities as eating? Current Muslim apologists often ridicule the "inferior Christian conception of God" and quote liberal Christian scholars to support their teachings about Jesus.

JESUS WAS NOT KILLED ON THE CROSS

Muslims insist that Jesus did not die on the cross. Some maintain that He was crucified but did not die. Others believe that just prior to His crucifixion, God substituted another man who looked like Jesus (perhaps Simon of Cyrene or Judas). The orthodox view suggests that Jesus was transported to heaven without dying.

> They ("who have received the Scriptures") have not believed on Jesus, and have spoken against Mary a grievous calumny, and have said, verily we have slain Christ Jesus the son of Mary, the apostle of God; yet they slew him not, neither crucified him, but he was represented by one in his likeness. . . . They did not really kill him: But God took him up into himself: and God is mighty and wise. (Qur'an 4:156-58)

Muslims may be divided in their understanding of the details surrounding the crucifixion record, but they speak with one voice when denying Jesus' death by crucifixion.

JESUS WILL OCCUPY A SIGNIFICANT PLACE ON THE LAST DAY

Tradition suggests that Jesus is now in an inferior level of paradise. At some future time, He will return to earth, reign for about forty years, marry, and father children. It is suggested that He will die and be buried in Medina, in a grave specially reserved for His remains. At the resurrection day, Jesus will rise from the dead and stand before God for judgment with all humanity.[2]

THE HOLY SPIRIT IS ONE OF THE TITLES OF THE ANGEL GABRIEL

Muslims identify the Holy Spirit with the angel Gabriel. This popular notion develops out of the names given to the angel in the Qur'an; chief among them is *the spirit.* Gabriel plays an extensive role in folk religion, and his name is often invoked to bring help to the needy. His name is often inscribed on talismans and charms.

> Verily we sent down the Qur'an in the night of Al Kadr. And what shall make thee understand how excellent the night of Al Kadr is? The night of Al Kadr is better than a thousand months. Therein do the angels descend and the spirit Gabriel also, by the permission of their Lord, with his decrees concerning every matter. (Qur'an 97:1-4)

JESUS FORETOLD THE COMING OF MUHAMMED

Muslims are anxious to establish some historical continuity between Islam, Judaism, and Christianity. That sense of continuity is particularly emphasized with regard to the prophets. Since Islam denies the biblical doctrine of the Holy Spirit, it is free to take the promises of the Spirit's coming and apply them to Muhammed. The Qur'an alludes to John 14:16-17, 25-26 and 16:7-11 when it says:

> And when Jesus the son of Mary said, O children of Israel, verily I am the apostle of God sent unto you confirming the law which was delivered before me and bringing good tidings of an apostle who shall come after me and whose name shall be Ahmad. (Qur'an 61:6)

In commenting on this text, Yusef Ali notes:[3]

Ahmad or Muhammad, the Praised One, is almost a translation of the Greek word Periclytos. In the present Gospel of John xiv.16, xv.26, and xvi.7, the word "Comforter" in the English version is for the Greek word "Paracletos," which means "Advocate," "one called to the help of another, a kind friend," rather than "Comforter." Our doctors contend that Paracletos is a corrupt reading for Periclytos, and that in their original saying of Jesus there was a prophecy of our holy Prophet Ahmad by name. Even if we read Paraclete, it would apply to the holy Prophet, who is "a Mercy for all creatures" (Qur'an 21:107) and "most kind and merciful to the Believers" (Qur'an 9:128).

The assertion that the Greek text consists of a corrupted reading is unsubstantiated by any rule or guideline of textual criticism. There is no doubt about the accuracy of *paracletos* (advocate) in the face of such conjecture.

CONTRASTS BETWEEN ISLAM AND CHRISTIANITY

There is a vast difference between correcting misunderstandings and coming to a knowledge of the truth in Christ. Once the confusion is understood, the deeper points of conflict stand out even more clearly. The following contrasts are systemic, woven into the very fabric of Muslim belief and conviction about life.

THE NATURE AND AUTHORITY OF HOLY BOOKS

The nature and scope of the Qur'an is very different from that of the Bible. Although both claim divine origin, the Bible claims to be the self-revelation of God; God can be known by finite man, though not with complete or exhaustive knowledge. By contrast, the Qur'an emphasizes the exclusive transcendence of God: He does not reveal Himself and consequently cannot be known or understood by anything in His creation. The Qur'an is largely concerned with how a man should live; submission and obedience are the key themes of Islam.

Although Muslims believe that the Bible is a holy book, they deny its authority and their obligation to obey its precepts. This conclusion is founded upon three convictions:

1. The Bible was superseded by the Qur'an, the last and greatest of the books given by God.
2. The Bible was corrupted by Jews and Christians to such an extent that it is no longer reliable.
3. Anything of enduring value about the history of the prophets or the message of earlier holy books has been incorporated into the Qur'an.

At the practical level, Muslims see no need to read the Bible since they believe that the Qur'an incorporates everything they need to understand or do in order to please God.

THE CHARACTER OF GOD

According to Islam, God is unique and transcendent in the absolute sense. Any theology that goes beyond absolute monotheism, including Trinitarianism, is considered *shirk* ("association"; by extension it means polytheism, making someone or something as the equal of God); this is the only sin that God will not forgive. Islam emphasizes absolute transcendence and sovereignty as the prime attributes of God; He can do anything He wishes, good or evil, without the moral restraint suggested by the attributes of love and holiness. God is essentially impersonal and unknowable, far distant from us and beyond comprehension. In contrast, the Bible teaches that God is a Triune being[4] and that Jesus reveals God so that all may know and enter into a relationship with God (cf. John 6:44; 14:6-11). It is helpful to remember that every objection to belief in a Triune God is based on the assumption that Christians really believe in three Gods. Keep this in mind and reply by showing where Muslims misunderstand your belief.

THE AUTHORITY OF JESUS AND MUHAMMED

Muslims affirm that Jesus was a great prophet, but nothing more. Muhammed is said to be the seal of the prophets; his authority is greater and supersedes the authority of Jesus. They not only contend that Jesus prophesied regarding Muhammed's coming, but that Muhammed's appearance was foretold in many ways. His work was accompanied by many clear signs, and his life was miraculous from beginning to end. The highest proof of his authority is the existence of the Qur'an. Muslims point to the Qur'an's beauty and majesty as beyond imitation, noting that Muhammed was regarded as illiterate. This is viewed as proof that the Qur'an came from God and that Muhammed is His prophet.[5]

THE NATURE OF JESUS CHRIST

The Qur'an and Islamic traditions hold that Jesus' birth was miraculous (Qur'an 19:16-22; 21:91; 66:12), that He did great miracles,[6] and that He is alive in heaven and will return to earth. But He is strictly human, like Adam.

Muslims mistakenly assume that Christians affirm the sonship of Jesus in the natural sense of the word *son* (i.e., God had sexual relations with a woman in order to have a human son).[7] This is the worst of blasphemies to the Muslim. But that understanding is also blasphemy to the Christian. The Bible teaches that Jesus Christ is the Son from eternity, fully God and fully man, born in human flesh by a miracle of the Holy Spirit, not by physical procreation.

THE NATURE OF HUMANITY

God created people weak, but not sinful.[8] Through submission to the guidance provided by the Qur'an, and with the help of the Muslim Community, we can please God. People are constitutionally good but subject to external influences, so they need protection from evil and education in what is good. Some Muslims also believe that Muhammed will intercede for them on the day of judgment. The Bible teaches that we were created for perfect fellowship with God. Through Adam's disobedience, we fell into sin and are incapable of any effort that would result in God's favor. Humanity is spiritually dead and unable to save itself.

THE NATURE AND MEANS OF SALVATION

In Islam, the responsibility for salvation is often thought to be collective; it naturally seeks to create a Muslim state that is united and universal. That societal setting enables people to save themselves by doing good works, so long as they are among the true believers and not among those who associate equals with God. In contrast, the Bible teaches that we cannot be saved apart from the imputation of our sin to Christ and a corresponding imputation of Christ's righteousness to us. The application of Christ's atoning sacrifice is by faith. This entire process is the result of God's grace, entirely apart from our personal effort.

FOR REFLECTION

1. What do you consider to be the main points of conflict between Islam and Christianity? Why are these issues so important?
2. How would you begin to answer the popular contention that Christians believe in three gods? What passages of Scripture could you choose to support your response?
3. Compare the Muslim and Christian conceptions of the relationship between God and people. What are the significant points of disagreement?
4. Muslims value Jesus highly, as one of the greatest among God's prophets. In what ways are the Muslim views of Jesus close to the teaching of the Bible? How are they different? How significant are those differences?
5. How does a Muslim's conception of God affect his self-image and appreciation of others?
6. How does the thinking of your Muslim friend compare with the information in this chapter? Does your friend share the same confusion and misconceptions? How does your friend think differently?

Part 2

The Christian Answer

CHAPTER SEVEN

DEVELOPING ANSWERS TO MUSLIM QUESTIONS

A man finds joy in giving an apt reply—
and how good is a timely word!
Proverbs 15:23

Now we turn to answers for Muslim objections. This chapter and those which follow are not intended to replace your reference tools on Christian theology, nor are they a substitute for reading the Qur'an and solid Christian books about ministry to Muslims. They are a beginner's palette with a few colors of paint that we can try. Do not be surprised if some parts are written more for you than for your Muslim friends. There is more art in the painter than in the paint.

But first, consider a question often pondered by Muslims: "Is this Christian really listening to me?" Loving listening sends a powerful answer. When you listen in love, you are listening as God listens. He may help you to hear unspoken questions. Good listening is part of becoming people who speak "only what is helpful for building others up *according to their needs,* that it may benefit those who listen" (Ephesians 4:29b, italics added).

FORMS FOR OUR ANSWERS

There is a difference between the *thing we mean* and the various *cultural forms* that give it a body. Translating the Bible comes naturally to us. But a purely traditional Muslim assumes that meaning is inseparably attached to form. We need to remember that many Muslims have a traditional religious culture even though other aspects of life have been modernized: new ideas settle in the valleys of the mind, whereas ancient tribes still rule the wooded hills.

Which *forms* or *terms* should you use, Christian or Muslim? Special Christian terms are accurate, but only to us; even if Muslims are willing to learn our terms, those words will still lack depth and emotional content for them. On the other hand, many of their expressions are warm and powerful but often carry a range of meaning we do not want. Effective communication requires both their terms and ours. Pray and risk using their language. Try some warmth. Tisdall suggests, "Use his own theological terms as far as possible, making quite sure that you fully understand them."[1]

TRADITIONAL AND WESTERN PROBLEMS

Traditional problems need traditional answers that are specific to Islam; this book will help you get started. But traditional Muslims may also rely on the documentary hypothesis and redaction criticism of the Bible, the scholarship of liberal Christianity. They think that such unbelief is normal Christianity. They do not stop to consider that applying the same methods of higher criticism to the Qur'an would destroy it.

For problems from Western philosophy or biblical criticism, we should turn to Western scholars for help. A handbook on alleged biblical discrepancies will prove indispensible.[2] A number of Christian publishers offer stimulating treatments of modern thought. Explore them carefully.

The challenge is to speak not just to *a* Muslim, but to *the* Muslim in front of us, with all of his or her varied experience and personal understandings. None of us can do the job alone; but each of us can contribute something.

ACTION IS AN ANSWER

Words and actions depend on each other for meaning. All of life is "show and tell." Our answers are heard in the context of how we are acting in the immediate situation, and in the broader context of our lifestyle. Your Muslim friend may know what makes you tick better than you do. Jesus underscored the relationship between words and actions: "Do not believe me unless I do what my Father does" (John 10:37). *Show* and *tell.* The apostle John also put them together: "This is the message we have heard from him and declare to you: God is light; in him there is no darkness at all." That is *tell.* "If we claim to fellowship with him yet walk in the darkness, we lie and do not live by the truth" (1 John 1:5-6). That is *show.* And that is communication: showing and telling about God's character and about how we relate to Him.

> But in your hearts set apart Christ as Lord. Always be prepared to give an answer to everyone who asks you to give the reason for the hope that you have. But do this with gentleness and respect, keeping a clear conscience, so that those who speak maliciously against your good behavior in Christ may be ashamed of their slander. (1 Peter 3:15 16)

FOR REFLECTION

1. How do you respond when a person's words and actions do not seem to fit together? To which do you give greatest credibility? Is this a special problem when the person is from a different cultural background?

2. Have you ever found it hard to believe that Christians from very distant cultural backgrounds are true believers just like you? Why?

3. How can you clearly demonstrate the reality of the gospel at work in your own life?

CHAPTER EIGHT

THE QUR'AN AND ISLAMIC TRADITION

WHAT SHALL WE DO WITH THE QUR'AN?

What do you think about the Qur'an? This question must be answered many times and in many different situations; you may find that you answer it differently as time goes by. It is an emotionally charged issue. It is important to our ministry, of course, but do not ignore the fact that it is also important to our feeling of who we are. When we feel the pressure of adapting to Muslims around us, we may be tempted to (1) remain in the safe and familiar realm of our own Christian culture, or (2) gain Muslim approval by identifying uncritically with their whole religious culture. For most of us, the first is probably the greater danger. But either extreme can kill our effective witness.

These tough decisions can be made appropriately. The eternal Son took the form of a servant. Culturally, He became a specific man with a specific social role. Paul made it his policy to become all things to all men (1 Corinthians 9:19-23), and in his varied ministry he adopted as many styles as he had audiences. John the Baptizer came as a Nazirite. All of these styles involved risk. All of them offended some people, but all of them communicated powerfully. Here are some possible approaches, along with comments. You may discover that different styles fit different situations.

Nazarite

ACCEPT THE DIVINE ORIGIN OF THE QUR'AN

The first alternative acknowledges that God is the source of the Qur'an, but it understands the Qur'anic message from a Christian perspective. This may please your Muslim friends, at least until they realize that you are approaching the Qur'an from a viewpoint that is foreign to the Qur'an itself. This approach is ruled out by our commitment to the Bible as the only rule of faith and life. The delicate and important task with all of these approaches is to let your friend know, at the right moment, that you do not accept the Qur'an as a book of heavenly origin. If you did, you would be a Muslim.

ARGUE FROM THE QUR'AN

Frame your argument in a Qur'anic context. This takes advantage of the Muslim's view of the authoritative nature of the Qur'an. It does not indicate your personal conviction. For example: "If you reject the Bible, you are also rejecting what the Qur'an says about the Bible." This approach has been used with some effectiveness among Muslims who are not willing to hear the Bible because they refuse any authority but the Qur'an.[1] It is possible to present the gospel during the course of such a discussion, but few prefer this option exclusively. Since it requires some expertise in the Qur'an, this pattern is unsuitable for beginners as a main line of approach.

APPEAL TO TRUTHS RECOGNIZED IN THE QUR'AN

All human culture reflects who we are, how we need God, and how we try to satisfy that need apart from Him. The familiar expressions of the Qur'an may be a standard cultural way of stating generally recognized truths with which Christians fully agree. Paul used this approach on Mars hill (Acts 17). You may learn much from the Qur'an about people and life. For example, consider some of the statements about God's sovereignty (cp. Qur'an 3:26-27 with Daniel 2:20-21), kindness and forgiveness (cp. Qur'an 2:263 with Hosea 6:6), trust in God (cp. Qur'an 3:38 with Isaiah 44:17-18 and 1 Samuel 5), hypocrisy (cp. Qur'an 107 with Matthew

6:5; 23:27-28), and false oaths (cp. Qur'an 2:224 with Mark 7:9-13 and Matthew 5:33-37).

IGNORE THE QUR'AN

You may choose to ignore the Qur'an or simply refuse to discuss what it says. There are some situations in which this is the best choice. Our Lord did not allow others to take control of a conversation. But it would be disastrous to ignore the Qur'an *all* of the time. Why? People may hear you say: "What I think is important and true; what you think is unimportant, and although I don't know much about it, I am not willing to discuss it." With some Muslims, your credibility will evaporate. And a whole area of their thinking will remain untouched by the gospel.

LEARN FROM THE QUR'AN

This is basic. If we are not learning, we are not only showing disinterest in what is important to many Muslims, but we are depriving ourselves of one of the richest funds of religious ideas, terms, and illustrations to be found in Arab Muslim culture. For example, everyday speech is salted with the repetition of *inshallah,* "if God wills," whenever plans or hopes are expressed; this pattern flows out of Qur'an 18:24-25 and a conviction about the sovereignty of God.

If you are studying and using Arabic, there are vast areas of life touched by the language and thought of the Qur'an. If it comes out naturally in your speech, it is one more way in which you are like them. Your message comes closer; it is more of a challenge. If your Muslim friends do not know or care much about the Qur'an, showing some knowledge may actually allow you to move quickly onto subjects that are closer to the heart.

HELP MUSLIMS FACE THE INTERNAL PROBLEMS OF THE QUR'AN

Is the Qur'an sometimes ambiguous or conflicting in its teaching? Does it contain errors of fact and language? Muslims need to realize this. One experienced worker says,

I like Taha Hussein's quote: "Give me a red pen so I can use it to correct the Qur'an." His opposition is widely known by students. They now tell me, "Yes, but he repented later in life." I sometimes ask them, "Why? Under duress?" Obviously you can get lost here, but I just touch on it, without arguing.

And if the Qur'an isn't plain on a given subject, suggest reading the Bible on the same matter. Life issues (e.g., marriage, child-rearing, friendship, money) can serve as excellent introductions to the Bible's storehouse of divine wisdom.

POINT OUT THE SIGNPOSTS IN THE QUR'AN

There are many places where the Qur'an could direct its readers to Christ, the Bible, and Christians. Fragments of Judaism and Christianity have been taken up in Islam, rather like pillars from ancient churches that have been incorporated into the construction of a mosque. They show up as Bible stories, teachings, words, and expressions. Of course they have a different meaning in the context of the Qur'an, but we can look at them from other perspectives, and ask: "To what does this point?" These serve as a starting point. The testimonies of some converts tell of the grace of God working through things found in the Qur'an.

BE WHAT ONLY THE REAL THING CAN BE

Some Muslims assume that the Qur'an is so convincing that if Christians could read Arabic and appreciate it, many of them would be converted to Islam. So what are they to make of a person who knows the Qur'an well but finds rich nourishment and delight in the Bible? Read the Qur'an with understanding and insight. But find your spiritual strength in the Bible and let that show through for your Muslim friend.

WHAT SHALL WE DO WITH MUSLIM TRADITION?

Muslims draw from an ocean of traditions about what the Prophet said and did. There are many questions the Qur'an doesn't answer, so the traditions serve as a supplement to the

Qur'an. Traditions also help to explain the Qur'an, and they support its authority by providing background.

You can learn from Muslim tradition. Read some of the traditions in an English translation to get an idea of what they are like. Tradition is a whole field of Islamic culture, and awareness will help you understand many beliefs and practices. If you learn Arabic, you will soon notice that preachers and writers often quote the traditions of the Prophet in sermons and books to support the point being made. Some of those quotations are striking and memorable.

So how should you deal with tradition? If a tradition is used to challenge the authority of Christ and the Bible, point out that tradition is like a garden in which the new plants have overwhelmed the original ones; it is very hard to tell which ones were there at the beginning. This is not a specific attack against Islam, but a problem common to many religions. The key question is, How do we know which traditions are authentic? Islam has many contradicting traditions; those widely received as being valid may not be the most authentic ones.[2]

FOR REFLECTION

1. Which of the approaches described here have you tried already? Which would you like to adopt in the future?
2. How does the Qur'an function, directly and indirectly, in the lives of Muslims you know? What satisfaction does it provide?
3. The force of tradition is different in evangelical Christianity and Islam. What are those differences? How will your attitude toward tradition affect your communication?

CHAPTER NINE

THE BIBLE AND MUSLIM OBJECTIONS

A Muslim who hesitates to read the Bible may, of course, be bound by the same fear or spiritual laziness that keeps many Christians from reading the Bible. Most have been taught by example to avoid the Bible. They may offer the excuses of annulment and corruption. But sometimes curiosity and spiritual hunger are very much alive.

What do Muslims learn from our behavior about the Bible's authority and authenticity? Do we read Scripture to hear the voice of God, or do we read in order to fulfill a religious rite? Do we explore it as a professional tool, or because it is the key to reality? What about meditation? And memorization? These issues affect our credibility. In general, Muslims who claim the ability to teach their religion can draw on a large fund of memorized Qur'an and tradition. Their standards of accuracy in memorization are high.

THE QUR'AN, THE BIBLE, AND CULTURE

Cross-cultural problems can be acute when we come to the Bible. Many traditional Muslims very naturally expect the Bible to be a sort of Christian Qur'an. Or at least they assume that the original Torah and Gospel were like the Qur'an. They may be repelled when they learn that a Christian does not bother to make himself pure in body (as well as thought) before touching the Bible. And they may never have thought about the problems involved in using translations.

Then there is the language and literary form of the Bible as it exists in Arabic translations. The expected signs of inspiration are missing. Where is the beautiful language of the Qur'an, with its music of reverence and worship? Where is the *bismillah,* those resonant words translated "in the name of God, the Merciful, the Compassionate"? In the Qur'an, the speaker is usually God, and the range of style is much narrower than in the Bible. To the Muslim, the Bible may seem like a jumble of traditional stories (more like the Hadith than the Qur'an), Zionist poetry, and letters from the early history of the church. Muslims expect eloquent, forceful preaching. How can Christians think this is "the speech of Allah"?

☐ A devout Muslim came to a Christian-Muslim discussion in a student center in Grenoble, France. Views were exchanged for a good while, and then he asked to say one last thing. He opened his Qur'an and read the poetically moving first chapter. He obviously felt its power and beauty, and thought that *the word of God* would be the final argument, convincing all who where present.

THE INSPIRATION OF THE BIBLE

Christians believe that God guided people to speak and write using their own thoughts and language, in forms adapted to a wide variety of people and situations. The prophets were carried along by the Holy Spirit (2 Peter 1:21) in a way that fully used their abilities rather than bypassing them; the product or writing is fully inspired.[1] The result is exactly what is needed to communicate God's message to people in many ages and cultures. A sophisticated student may understand this without much trouble. A modernized Muslim who has rejected his religion may not care. But for a person of limited education who has never left the rural setting, or for a city person who is rediscovering his identity in terms of the Islamic heritage, the barrier may still seem unsurmountable.

THE STYLE OF THE BIBLE

The style of the Bible is often held against the message, as if it were self-evident that a style that differs from the Qur'an provides sufficient reason to suspect that there is something wrong with the message. Professor Ahmed Hussein introduced a series of articles on the Bible by speaking of the two copies of the Bible in his library. The names of the translators are not given, "but what is certain is that the style of both translations is colorless, to the point that this colorlessness has become the distinguishing and unifying stamp of any translation of the Bible."[2] Those of us who have absorbed the traditional Christian style from the days of our first contact with Arabic will not feel the problem like those who drink in the music of the Qur'an with their mother's milk and learn in school to treasure its poetic power.

When you use Arabic translations, remember the importance of the atmosphere. Most Arabic translations have deliberately avoided Qur'anic forms, even though Qur'anic forms are the means by which most Muslims think and feel deeply about God. Some recent translations have a more attractive style, but they have not been widely adopted among evangelicals. A great deal will depend on the religious culture of your Muslim friends; their needs vary widely. There is no path in translation that will guarantee acceptance: antagonistic Muslims may cry out against a heavily Islamic translation as an attempt to imitate the inimitable Qur'an, while rejecting other translations as inferior in style.[3]

An apparent cultural problem can, of course, hide a dozen spiritual problems. But the reverse is also true and the two are interwoven.

HAS THE BIBLE BEEN ANNULLED?

Many Muslims say that the Bible is no longer applicable. The simplest form of this theory may be put this way:

As the *Injil* (Gospel) abrogated the *Tawrat* (Torah) of Moses, so the Qur'an abrogated the *Injil. Abrogation* means declaring it null, void, or unnecessary. Therefore, even if genuine copies of the former books exist, there is no need for Muslims to read them.

At the practical level, when asked about reading the Bible, some may say: "Yes, I've read the Bible." But when pressed, what they *mean* is that they have read all they need of it *in the Qur'an.*

To some Muslims, this may seem like the easiest and best way to answer someone who asks why they do not read the Bible. You may find it used by those who know little about Christianity and wish to avoid embarrassment or confrontation, or who simply do not want to discuss the matter. Most have not thought it through. This view is contrary to both the Bible and the Qur'an.

DOES THE BIBLE CLAIM THAT IT WILL BE ANNULLED?

If the Sovereign God intended to send the Qur'an to replace the Bible, it would be natural to expect that the Bible would mention its own abrogation. But there is no such teaching in the Bible.

We freely admit great changes in the historical situation that some may point to as indications of annulment. But this means that some earlier revelation does not apply *in the same way;* that is very different from suggesting that it does not apply at all. For instance, the Mosaic law was given as the regulating code during a specific period of history. When Christ died, our relationship to the Mosaic law changed radically (Galatians 2:15-22; see also Romans 7; Ephesians 2:15; Hebrews 8). But the Mosaic law continues to actively reveal God's holy character and teach us how to live. On a smaller scale, some directions were meant for specific circumstances. For example, Christ first instructed His disciples to rely on the support of those who received the message; later He warned them that they could no longer expect such help (Luke 9:3; 22:35-38). So it is evident that certain statements were originally intended for a limited period. But otherwise, the Word of God is valid for all eternity.

The entire Bible speaks to us with full authority and relevance (2 Timothy 3:16). As someone familiar with the Bible, you can honestly say that there is no indication that any part of it will be annulled.

THE BIBLE AND FULFILLMENT

In replying to the charge that the Bible has been annulled, Christians often use Matthew 5:17-18, where Christ said:

Do not think that I have come to abolish the Law or the Prophets; I have not come to abolish them but to fulfill them. I tell you the truth, until heaven and earth disappear, not the smallest letter, not the least stroke of a pen, will by any means disappear from the Law until everything is accomplished.

Abolish refers to abrogation. Christ did not come to annul or repeal the Mosaic law. He did come to fulfill it. The context makes clear that Christ fulfills the law by providing its true meaning and perfected form. Beyond the immediate context, you can see that Jesus fulfills the Mosaic law in other ways: (1) by accomplishing its requirements fully, both for himself and for us; and (2) by placing it under the wings, so to speak, of the New Covenant. It thus retires from the role of commanding outward details of daily life while establishing forever its role of revealing God in His holiness. What is true for the Mosaic law is true also for the prophets. "Until everything is accomplished" may be understood as referring to the end of history, or the fulfillment of all God's purpose. It is not a reference to the coming of Muhammed.

THE QUR'AN AND ABROGATION

The Qur'an applies the idea of abrogation to its own texts, not to those of the previous scriptures. This is the view of the great authorities within Islam.[4] The Qur'an speaks of abrogation in this way:

Such of Our revelations as We abrogate or cause to be forgotten, we bring (in place) one better or the like thereof. Knowest thou not that Allah is Able to do all things? (Qur'an 2:106)

In fact, Muslim scholars believe that many verses have been annulled, but there is great confusion over which ones.[5] Imagine the following conversation:

Christian: The verb *to annul* is used only twice in the Qur'an, and on each occasion, refers not to the Bible but to certain verses of the Qur'an itself, which are declared to be annulled. Your learned men declare that there are 225 verses thus annulled, though they are not agreed on which ones they are. Do you still read these annulled verses?

Muslim: We do, for we read the whole Qur'an.

Christian: If you read verses which the Qur'an states to be annulled, and think yourself bound to do so, why should you consider yourself free from the obligation to read the Ṭaurat and Injil, which the Qur'an does not declare to be annulled but commands you to believe? (Qur'an 2:130)

This argument is useful, but do not forget the personal dimension. One of the most helpful replies to the Bible's alleged abrogation is an honest testimony to God's use of the Bible in your own life. You can go on to ask, "What parts have you read? What did they mean to you?" A Muslim who has experienced the power of the Bible, applied by the Holy Spirit, will think differently about the issue of annulment.

HOW DOES THE QUR'AN VIEW THE BIBLE?

The Qur'an does not regard the Bible as a dead book. Sometimes the Qur'an appeals to the Torah and Gospel as an authority for life and doctrine. These texts lean hard against the idea of abrogation and the charge of corruption.

Lo! We did reveal the Torah, wherein is guidance and a light. . . . And We caused Jesus, Son of Mary, to follow in their footsteps, confirming that which was (revealed) before him, and We bestowed on him the Gospel wherein is guidance and a light, confirming that which was (revealed) before it. . . . Let the People of the Gospel judge by what Allah hath revealed therein. . . . And unto thee have We revealed the Scripture with the truth, confirming whatever Scripture was before it, and a watcher over it. . . . Say: O People of the Scripture! Ye have naught (of guidance) till ye observe the Torah and the Gospel and that which was revealed unto you from your Lord. (Qur'an 5:44-68)

And if thou (Muhammed) art in doubt concerning that which We have revealed unto thee, then question those who read the Scripture (that was) before thee. Verily the Truth from thy Lord hath come unto thee. So be not of the waverers. (Qur'an 10:95)

If the Bible's authority is accepted, even on the basis of the teachings of the Qur'an, one must also accept that the Gospel is final. The Bible makes clear that further revelation cannot go beyond Christ, it can only reveal more of Him. Underscore the uniqueness of Christ. A Muslim may begin to understand this through the idea of the Word (John 1:17-18; see also Ephesians 1:21). Christ is the eternal Son, the heir of all things, who stands in contrast to the succession of mortal prophets and priests who preceded Him (Hebrews 1:1-4). This is familiar language to Muslims. At many levels, Islam is a return to the culture and, superficially, to the content of the Old Testament.

To know the Christ of the Bible is to discover that He is not merely a last step in the history of revelation but the summing up of all history. Your friend may be slow to accept this, but you can report it. This allows your friend to see a bit of the Christian vision of history. Colossians 1 may help one who is seeking; if your friend continues reading into chapter 2, which combats legalistic and occultic views, so much the better!

HAS THE BIBLE BEEN CORRUPTED?

Jesus said, "Heaven and earth will pass away, but my words will never pass away" (Matthew 24:35). "Never?" says the Muslim. "I'm sorry to tell you that it has already happened."

A Muslim believes that the Qur'an is right. It repeatedly refers to the *Taurat* (Torah), the *Zabur* (Psalms), and the *Injil* (Gospel) as revealed books and requires faith in them. But what if the Bible does not agree with the Qur'an? Obviously, Muslims think, someone is misquoting the Bible or, as most of them are taught, tampering with the text.[6] If this is a genuine problem to your friend, it has some very practical implications:

- It may help if a Muslim can actually *see* the text you are quoting.
- A few traditional Muslims may be afraid that a corrupted text will corrupt their thinking.
- Your Muslim friend may think that arguments from the Bible need not have any weight, for the text has been altered.

>If the text has been altered to support Christian teaching, would not Christians unknowingly argue from precisely those texts which have been changed?

Problems need not stop us from presenting Biblical truth *simply as truth* and allowing the Holy Spirit to bring conviction. A preacher once remarked: a sword is intended for use, not as a subject of debate. How often the Word penetrates *in spite* of a Muslim's initial attitude to it! Needless to say, the deeper our personal honesty, the greater God's delight as He uses us to bring conviction that the gospel is true.

CHARGES OF CORRUPTION

The basic accusation of corruption comes from two sources, which may be called traditional and modern. The *traditional* source claims that the text of the Bible has been changed almost beyond recognition. "That is why you have four gospels instead of one," a Muslim may say. Charges from traditional sources come from Muslims, but they are not soundly based on the Qur'an and the best tradition. The *modern* source adopts the conclusions of liberal religious scholars, who assert that the Torah was written long after Moses, that the Gospels display flagrant contradictions and are not reliable historically, and that Paul corrupted the original religion of Jesus. Increasingly, Muslim teachers are using the liberal conclusions to support traditional accusations.[7]

TRADITIONAL OBJECTIONS

When you read the Qur'an, it seems inescapable that *the authoritative Torah and Gospel were still in use in the time of Muhammed.* Detailed study of the Qur'an suggests that some Jews are accused of deliberately misreading the texts or distorting the message. Even if that charge were true, it is still not the same thing as changing the written text itself. The Qur'an does not actually accuse Christians of tampering with the text. There are a large number of Qur'anic texts involved that are adequately treated elsewhere, so they will not be considered.[8] A Muslim who honestly considers Islamic sources should, in fact, accept the authority of the Torah and Gospel as they existed in the time of Muhammed. If that is accepted, carefully present the fact that the oldest manuscripts of the Bible date from long before the death of Muhammed (A.D. 632). Be prepared to clarify your claim with explanation and back it up with some facts.

The Qur'anic texts cited earlier concerning abrogation also speak to the problem of corruption. In addition, consider:

> And argue not with the People of the Scripture unless it be in (a way) that is better, save with such of them as do wrong; and say: We believe in that which hath been revealed unto us and revealed unto you; our God and your God is One, and unto Him we surrender. (Qur'an 29:46)

There is also a line of Qur'anic teaching which suggests that God would not allow His own speech to be changed. These passages seem to go against both annulment and corruption:

> Those unto whom We gave the Scripture (aforetime) know that it is revealed from the Lord in truth. . . . Perfected is the Word of thy Lord in truth and justice. There is naught that can change His words. He is the Hearer, the Knower. (Qur'an 6:115-16)

> Theirs are good tidings in the life of the world and in the Hereafter —There is no changing the Words of Allah—that is the Supreme Triumph. (Qur'an 10:65)

A Muslim who honestly considers texts such as these may recognize that the Qur'an itself does not clearly support all of the traditional objections to the Bible. In fact, it provides reasons for rejecting them. However, the situation is complicated by the fact that some modern interpreters and translators of the Qur'an adopt interpretations that fail to bring this out.

Common sense often helps in handling the traditional objections. Things can be put very simply. For instance: If the Jews had corrupted their own books, would not they have also changed the awful things we read about them in the Torah and the Psalms? Do you really think that God, who is all-powerful, would allow His Word to be corrupted? And how would it have been possible to change the Gospel after copies were distributed? Imagine the problems of anyone who wanted to change yesterday's edition of a newspaper! And how credible is it that Jesus, Muhammed, or other capable leaders would choose as their followers people who, after the leader had left the scene, would do a complete turnaround and fatally distort their message?

Accusation alone provides no proof. Most Muslims have heard that the Bible has been changed. Denial by Christians isn't very convincing. After all, it stands to reason that Christian leaders would be out of a job if word got around that the Bible contains only shreds of the former revelation. But it may help your friend to realize that accusations are easy to make, but they must be supported by evidence. If the charge of corruption is true, where is the evidence? What changes were made? When? What are the early historical documents on which the charges are based? Remember that the object is not to silence your friends but to gently lead them into understanding the difference between an accusation and a demonstration of truth.

MODERN OBJECTIONS

Since this book is designed to help with problems specific to witness among Muslims, what follows is only a brief look at modern objections. A number of books are available to deal with the objections of liberal scholars. The bibliography suggests a few places to look. Sometimes, of course, the answer will come from an informed person rather than a book.

General principles. There are a few general principles that can help when you are faced with questions about such matters as scientific and historical errors, contradictions, authorship, and the date of writing.

1. We accept both the authority of the Bible and the authority of science. All truth is God's truth; there is no inconsistency if we get all the facts and interpretation right. If we cannot make the pieces fit, something is wrong. Few Muslims are accustomed to thinking like this; they tend to dismiss anything that does not fit with the Qur'an. The good news is that the Bible does not shrink or disappear when put in contact with the world of science, and science also

gets full justice. For example, the striking simplicity of the first chapters of Genesis are without parallel in heathen writings or the Qur'an. Notice how the story of humanity's Fall gives just what we need to understand the history of humanity and salvation, without the fanciful embroidery that so readily enters into tradition.[9]

2. As a result of the great secularization and freedom of Western societies, it is possible for people to attain high positions in the church and its institutions without holding to the historic Christian faith. Citing an authority is important to many Muslims. They may think that citing a "Christian authority" who doesn't believe the Bible is proof that the book is unreliable. But there is wide variation in what Western authorities say. There is a place for recognizing the authority of experts, but one must also consider their presuppositions and the nature of their expertise.

3. Muslim apologists often accept liberal conclusions without stopping to consider the assumptions that support them, and the accuracy of their scholarship. Typically, the miraculous element is ruled out. You may ask, what would result if the same criteria were applied to the study of the Qur'an?

4. Scientific criticism and biblical scholarship are always changing as new philosophies move to center stage. A shift in philosophy often leads to a new theory in science, changing the generally accepted picture of the world and the way facts are interpreted. To put it another way, new philosophy often *precedes* new science. This is the case with evolution, for instance.

5. Revolutionary new discoveries appear with regularity. Any scientific book that is in full agreement with current scholarship undoubtedly contains errors that will become obvious as time goes by. Before a young Arab shepherd discovered the Dead Sea Scrolls, liberal scholars estimated that the gospel of John was written late in the second century A.D.

6. Some apologists (both Muslim and Christian) are badly informed and fall into the trap of using any evidence or statement that appears to support their position. Your friends may have read an article that claims that science has found the *Shahada* (Confession) written in the human body. Or they may have read that there is a miraculous matching in the number of times certain words occur in the Qur'an. Much of the support is dubious. You need to sow some healthy doubt about quick fixes that "prove" the Qur'an (or the Bible). It is also a reminder not to use any source just because it sounds impressive. Muslims need to read a deep commitment to truth in us and in our sources.

7. We freely admit that the problems are very complex. This is only natural, for the Bible was given in widely different cultures and historical periods. Parts of it include older documents. We believe that God chose to work through the capacities of the writers, with all their varied personalities, gifts, and literary techniques, assuring a *perfect result* (which is not the same thing as a *perfect writer*).

The so-called real, historical Jesus and Paul. Some of the most famous names in Western scholarship have examined the New Testament through lenses containing a remarkable filter. Simply put, whatever is supernatural must be unhistorical, so it must be discarded. The filter is applied both to physical miracles and to the lives of Jesus and the apostles. The object is to remove the outer layers of myth, miracle story, church tradition, psychological processes, or whatever, and get down to the core of historical facts. An immense effort has been expended to rewrite the history of Christianity without the supernatural element.

In fairness to modern liberal scholarship, we recognize that people and ideas grew as revelation was added and pondered under the direction of the Spirit. We also acknowledge the existence of cultural factors and literary conventions. It is obvious that in the Bible God used people, words, and ideas to express His message. We ask our Muslim friends to join us in rejecting antisupernatural interpretations of the Bible.

Jesus has been the subject of various, and sometimes conflicting, antisupernatural interpretations. To show the false nature of these views would require a whole library. But consider one thought. I. Howard Marshall, discussing the shocking authority which with Jesus spoke as lawgiver, writes:

> The point to be observed here is that even the application of radical methods to the study of the Gospels leads us to this unavoidable characteristic of the ministry of Jesus. Somehow or other, Jesus still manages to get through the most rigid critical barriers. We must, however, ask whether this radical picture of Jesus rests on a correct reading of the sources, and also whether the evidence does not take us somewhat further.[10]

Paul is interesting to Muslims because of his immense influence in the history of the church and because he represents a possible explanation of how the church came to give Jesus such an exalted position. Two things must be said. First, Paul based his claim to authority on new revelation: the risen Christ personally appeared to him and showed him things that had never been revealed before. Now this claim to new revelation may seem like unsupported pretension. But second, the other apostles and leaders, who had been with Jesus, knew Paul; *they fully recognized his call and apostolic authority.* If Peter accepted Paul, who are we to refuse him? Galatians and Acts tell much of the story; they have the ring of history since Peter is not always placed in a favorable light.

DOES THE BIBLE CONTRADICT ITSELF?

Contradictions, especially in the Gospels, are an increasingly popular excuse for dismissing the Bible. You may find this issue in the mouth of a Muslim apologist, or as a problem expressed by a Muslim who is beginning to study the Bible. One Muslim correspondent put it this way:

> I believe in the books which God revealed through His apostles, including the Psalms, the Torah, the Gospel, and the Qur'an. But God has informed us, through our lord Muhammad, that the Torah and the

Gospel were exposed to corruption and falsification. It is written in the
Chapter of the Cow [2:79], "Therefore woe be unto those who write
the Scripture with their hands and then say, "This is from Allah," that
they may purchase a small gain therewith. Woe unto them for that
their hands have written, and woe unto them for that they earn thereby." . . .

Surely God has spoken the truth! And there are many verses on
this subject. But this saying seems cheap if it is not supported by evidence and proofs which substantiate its truth, and the Qur'an gives us
the key: "Will they not then ponder on the Qur'an? If it had been from
other than Allah they would have found therein much incongruity."
That is, the standard and criterion on which we must base our claim
that a book is from God, is that it is free of contradiction and
incongruity.[11]

How can we help Muslims who take an approach like this?
Personal honesty is very important. Yes, there are problems. But
they are relatively small ones, and they do not affect the message.
It helps to remember these factors:

- God guided the writers to select the things that were appropriate to the needs of their audience and their purpose in
  writing.
- When we compare parallel passages, it can be difficult to
  tell whether we are dealing with one original event or two
  similar events. There is natural similarity in the events, because the same kind of thing was done so often in similar
  circumstances. There also may be natural similarity in accounts of different events, because some ways of presenting the facts are more helpful and memorable than others.
  As a result, it is difficult to reconstruct the history.
- Problems remain in harmonizing the gospels. But the very
  presence of problems is strong testimony to the fact that
  Christians did not tamper with the text. These problems
  are not of recent discovery. Parallel passages have been
  studied since the early centuries of Christianity. For example, in the fourth century A.D., Eusebius of Caesarea developed an elaborate numbering system for finding them. It is
  the current attitude of unbelief that is different.

- The Qur'an is one book, from one source, written down in a short period of time. Yet it also has problems.[12] Now open a Bible and look at the table of contents. It is composed of many books, written down by many authors over many years. It is only natural that the number of problems should be greater in the case of the Bible. The unity of the message in spite of the diversity of sources makes the message even more remarkable and worthy of belief.
- God knew all about the problems, yet determined to communicate His Word anyway. Why not ask your Muslim friend to join in a search for the answer? Even if the question remains unanswered, the search involves discovering the message of the passages involved.[13]

Keep the problem of alleged contradictions in perspective. For a really serious case of contradictions, compare the Bible and the Qur'an. Some manuscripts of the Bible are much older than the Qur'an. When the Qur'an, centuries later, gives a different version of a story (such as that of Joseph), a different message about Christ, and a different message about what God is like, why should we accept the later book as being the original version of the message?

WHAT ABOUT THE GOSPEL OF BARNABAS?

Many Muslims believe that there is a true gospel that has survived, the Gospel of Barnabas. This false gospel should not be confused with the Epistle of Barnabas.[14] Here are some selections from the English translation of the Gospel of Barnabas:[15]

> Barnabas, apostle of Jesus the Nazarene, called Christ, to all them that dwell upon the earth desireth peace and consolation.
> Dearly beloved, the great and wonderful God hath during these past days visited us by his prophet Jesus Christ in great mercy of teaching and miracles, by reason whereof many, being deceived of Satan, under pretense of piety, are preaching most impious doctrine, calling Jesus son of God, repudiating the circumcision ordained of God for ever, and permitting every unclean meat: among whom also Paul hath been deceived, whereof I speak not without grief; for which

cause I am writing that truth which I have seen and heard, in the intercourse that I have had with Jesus, in order that ye may be saved. (p. 2)

Jesus answered, "Philip, God is a good without which there is naught good; God is a being without which there is naught that is; God is a life without which there is naught that liveth." (p. 17)

Jesus answered: "This faithless generation seek [sic] a sign, but it shall not be given them, because no prophet is received in his own country." (p. 23)

[Jesus, in recounting the story of Adam, says,] "Adam, having sprung up upon his feet, saw in the air a writing that shone like the sun, which said: 'There is only one God, and Mohammad is the messenger of God.'" (p. 50)

Then said he who writeth: "Daniel the prophet, describing the history of the kings of Israel and their tyrants, writeth thus: 'The king of Israel joined himself with the king of Judah to fight against the sons of Belial (that is, reprobates) who were the Ammonites . . . '." (p. 207)

Jesus answered " . . . God, in order that I be not mocked of the demons on the day of judgement, hath willed that I be mocked of men in this world by the death of Judas, making all men to believe that I died upon the cross. And this mocking shall continue until the advent of Mohammad, the messenger of God, who, when he shall come, shall reveal this deception to those who believe God's law." (p. 271)

English and Arabic editions of this pseudo-gospel exist, but few Muslims have read it. If they had, they would not be quick to claim it as a true gospel, for although it is written to support Islam, a number of things in it disagree with the Qur'an. It is a mixture of quotations and adaptations from the Bible, especially the Gospels, with later materials. It is out of touch with the world of the first century. Responsible scholars who have studied the manuscripts, the language, and the thought of this pseudo-gospel, suggest that it was probably written after A.D. 1300. It obviously does not date from the first century.[16]

Muslims may benefit from learning more about the Gospel of Barnabas if it introduces some healthy doubt as to the credibility of sources on which they have relied. Perhaps they will realize that there are such things as false gospels and that one was made by someone who writes like an ill-informed Muslim. Informed

Muslim apologists will not often use this pseudo-gospel in debate with Christians. If the Crusades are like a dead and twisted tree, you may think of this book as a bitter fruit that grew after most of the leaves had fallen. The Gospel of Barnabas is indigestible to Muslim and Christian alike.

TEXTUAL CRITICISM

You should know something about the science of textual criticism. The following discussion is abbreviated and simplified. Examine the bibliography for helpful resource tools. Since Islam is primarily based on a book, you must be well grounded in this area; the Christian-Muslim debate is heating up in Europe and North America, as well as in Muslim lands.

Manuscripts differ from each other, and the variations mark out *families* of manuscripts with similar readings. By comparing the manuscripts, with an eye to history and geography, it is possible to reconstruct a history of various types of texts, somewhat akin to tracing your family's genealogy. Analyzing how scribes copied manuscripts, observing how they made changes that we *know* are mistakes, gives scholars background when comparing texts that are puzzling. One simple rule is that the original text is the one that best explains how the other readings came into existence. Textual critics are experts, but their expertise does not mean that they agree on every detail of the text. As for the New Testament, most evangelical scholars weigh readings from all text types before making a decision. This results in an *eclectic text,* represented in English translations such as the *Revised Standard, New International,* and *New American Standard* versions. A minority of evangelical scholars hold that one particular text type, the *majority text*, is the true one; this text underlies the King James, or Authorized Version. The majority text summarizes most of the existing manuscripts of the New Testament. However, the bulk of existing manuscripts were made long after the earliest ones available.

THE TEXT OF THE BIBLE

If your Muslim friend raises questions about a doubtful text, it will probably come from the Gospels. The following texts are frequently mentioned: Mark 16:9-20; John 5:3b-4; John 7:53–8:11; 1 Timothy 3:16; and 1 John 5:7b-8a (except for 1 Timothy 3:16, in the *New International Version* these verses are either accompanied by an explanatory note or are given only in the margin).

Textual criticism has established the text of Scripture with a very high degree of certainty. Some scholars estimate that about 1 percent remains in doubt. For your work with Muslims, remember that even when the true text is in doubt, *we know the range of possibilities* (i.e., the different readings suggested for a text), and there is little difference in meaning. No important doctrine of the Bible is in doubt.

The preceding comments apply mostly to the New Testament. The history, transmission, and establishment of the Old Testament text is slightly different. In brief, the Dead Sea Scrolls provide solid evidence that the biblical text was written well before most liberal scholars had speculated. An Isaiah scroll, copied about 150 B.C., contains clear prophecy about Christ and affirms key truths that Muslims need to acknowledge.

The usual policy in Arabic Bible translations has been to give no indication that any part of the text is doubtful. This may be a convenient omission during early conversations, but to imply that there are no problems dangerously contradicts reality. Muslim sources constantly charge that the Bible has been changed. If your friends discover that you are hiding the truth about textual problems, why should they trust you regarding the truth of the gospel? Learn to deal with these issues in an honest and forthright manner.

THE TEXT OF THE QUR'AN

There are fewer variations in the text of the Qur'an than in the Bible. This is not surprising since the Qur'an is only one book, given over a single generation. It is also because very early in the history of the text of the Qur'an, before the great spread of Islam, *variant copies were destroyed* and a single text established. So it is impossible to compare the differences that existed in the early years of Islam. Only a few minor variants remain.[17] John Gilchrist, in his booklet *The Textual History of the Qur'an and the Bible,*[18] tells about the number of variants and the destruction of manuscripts. He suggests that the current Qur'anic text is not the best one. Since most Muslims believe that there are no problems at all with the text of the Qur'an, or at most only a few different readings of the vowels, this material can provide the healthy shock of reality.

FOR REFLECTION

1. How do people you know choose a translation of the Bible? Of the Qur'an?
2. Suppose that you are giving your Muslim friend a Bible. You want to include a one-page letter of explanation and help. What ideas would you mention?
3. Allegations about the Bible's corruption are bound to arise in your conversations. How will you respond to those questions? How would you characterize the tone of your response (i.e., defensive, uncertain, argumentative, and so on)?
4. Develop responses to the allegations raised with regard to doubtful texts in the Gospels (Mark 16:9-20; John 5:3*b*-4; 7:53–8:11).

CHAPTER TEN

THE DOCTRINE
OF GOD

Wo cannot know God fully, but He has shown us something of Himself, and this something can be described in the words "You are good, and what you do is good; teach me your decrees" (Psalm 119:68). Like Christians, Muslims speak of the attributes (*Sifaat*) of God. Some recite His ninety-nine names, using a rosary. They may call out to God using His names (e.g., O Forgiving One!). The expression *bismillah arrahmaan arrahiim* (in the name of God the Merciful, the Compassionate) comes at the head of many of their speeches and documents, and *allahu 'akbar* (God is Most Great!) is heard with every call to prayer.

THE ATTRIBUTES OF GOD

Christians and Muslims alike have problems when they think about God's attributes. One Christian worker recalls:

> Berrada was a doctoral candidate in a French university. He stared at me intensely waiting for an answer to his question: "The Qur'an says that God is merciful and compassionate; also that he is severe in punishment. How do you reconcile these two?"
>
> It was significant that Berrada was practically an agnostic! But the question remains. When God is both just and the justifier of sin-

ners (Romans 4), then the two traits are joined. This is displayed at the cross, and only there.

Does this common struggle for understanding say anything about the content of your answers? To some extent, Muslims and Christians have a common fund of words and ideas. This is limited by the Muslim tendency (exaggerated by theologians) to make God so unknowable that His names become mere counters that tell us nothing about reality. But practically speaking, you cannot doubt that God's attributes are a source of comfort and satisfaction to many ordinary Muslims. Consider emphasizing these points:

- God is knowable, not merely in some abstract sense, but in the dynamic, interactive way He reveals himself as a Person, in the kind of close relationship described by the language of love, family, friendship, and marriage. Abraham, whom Muslims know as "the friend of God," clearly illustrates appropriate intimacy with God. Note, however, that you should use caution in presenting love between man and woman as a help in understanding God's love.
- God acts, here and now. Not just upholding the world, but answering prayer and surprising us with His own fresh initiatives. His powerful saving work in Christ changes things now.
- God is not arbitrary; He is consistent with Himself. The cross shows us how God is holy, just, and loving, all at the same time. He is not loving at the expense of His justice. His internal consistency is clearly displayed in His activity.

What approaches might you take to help your Muslim friend understand the character of God? The way of communicating suggests a great deal about the message.

- Reassure him that Muslims and Christians hold many truths about God in common.
- Be open about your worship and devotional life. Because worship forms are different, Muslims may think that Chris-

tians have a poor, thin idea of God and a starving worship experience. Be clear about your love for God and desire to submit to Him.

- Prayer can be important both for what God hears and for what your friends can observe. Show your relationship with God at work.

When you begin talking about God's names and attributes, you may quickly think that Muslims and Christians have much in common. But you will soon discover some of the most important differences between Christianity and Islam. For example, passages in the gospel of John reveal qualities such as humility and obedience within God Himself. These are close to the heart of the good news, and tragically far from the mind of Muslims.

THE TRINITY

Muslims are often confused by what they think Christians believe. This is clearly illustrated in a letter from a radio listener:

> I am an Algerian by nationality, and I profess the religion of Islam. . . . As for the Christian religion, as I know, it professes [faith] in the Trinity (The Father, the Mother, and the Son), and that the Son is *'Isa al-MasiiH* (on whom be peace).[1]

This is the same confusion about the Trinity discussed earlier. Remember that a Muslim uses the term *Holy Spirit* to refer to the angel Gabriel, who supposedly delivered the revelation of the Qur'an to Muhammed. In the Qur'an, Christians are warned and told by God not to say "Three" (Qur'an 4:171).

It is obvious that what most Muslims reject is *not* the biblical teaching about the Trinity. Most have never heard the true Christian teaching stated, much less explained in a way they can understand. The situation is confused because some "Christians" venerate Mary. But that should not be held against the true biblical teaching, any more than we should hold the errors and superstitious practices of some Muslims against the Qur'an.

THE CHRISTIAN DOCTRINE OF THE TRINITY

In the Bible, the one and only true God reveals Himself as the Father, the Son, and the Holy Spirit. When Christians say that God "reveals Himself," we recognize that we are creatures and must depend on what He shows us and tells us about Himself. Although God gives us true knowledge about Himself, it is incomplete and cannot be reduced to our limited terms. We have true knowledge about God, but that knowledge is not exhaustive. Mystery should not surprise us.

A Muslim may object that the word *Trinity* is not in the Bible; but then the Muslim theological term for God's unity (*tawHid*) is not in the Qur'an either. Yet Muslims rightly accept the term because it is useful. Both terms give a comprehensive view, rather like a distant view of a landscape.

We believe in one God. From the beginning of your discussion, say emphatically and warmly, in terms a Muslim can appreciate, that there is only one God. This was declared in the Torah (Deuteronomy 6:4) and repeated by the prophets. Isaiah 44 is a gold mine of passionate *tawHid,* if a Muslim reader can adjust to Isaiah's way of saying it. Make the point that idolatry does not apply only to visible gods. Money, sex, success, and occult power are all popular gods. What are ours?

When Jesus came, He reaffirmed God's unity. He quoted the First Commandment with convicting power (Matthew 22:37; Mark 12:30; Luke 10:27). The New Testament Epistles, along with the history of the church, show that Christians (including people from many Arab lands) paid with their lives for refusing to worship any god but God. Beside your affirmation that God is one stands James's solemn warning: "You believe that there is one God. Good! Even the demons believe that—and shudder" (James 2:19). However, remember that according to Islamic teaching the jinn can be saved.

Three in one. There is only one God, yet in this one are three eternal distinctions, or Persons. God is not a vast uniformity, like empty space. Diversity has always been a part of the ultimate unity of Ultimate Being. Theologians say that there is only one essence or substance of God. Yet the Father, Son, and Spirit address each other as Persons and act toward each other in a manner that confirms that there are personal relationships between them. These relationships are not always symmetrical:

> Notwithstanding that the Father, Son, and Spirit are the same in substance and equal in power and glory, it is no less true, according to the Scriptures, that (a) the Father is first, the Son second, and the Spirit third; (b) the Son is of the Father, and the Spirit is of the Father and the Son; (c) the Father sends the Son, and the Father and the Son send the Spirit; and (d) the Father operates through the Son, and the Father and the Son operate through the Spirit. The converse of these statements is never found.[2]

When you get into serious conversations about the Trinity, refresh your memory with the early creeds. This is especially important if you live in the Middle East where there is a traditional Christian minority and the early creeds have great importance.

IMPORTANT PASSAGES IN THE BIBLE

Two central passages demand your attention: the baptism of Jesus and Matthew's record of the Great Commission. Just prior to Jesus' ascension to heaven, Matthew records:

> Then Jesus came to them and said, "All authority in heaven and on earth has been given to me. Therefore go and make disciples of all nations, baptizing them in the name of the Father and of the Son and of the Holy Spirit, and teaching them to obey everything I have commanded you." (Matthew 28:18-20a)

Notice that *the name* is singular. Some Middle Eastern Christians begin writings with the formula "In the name of the Father, the Son, and the Holy Spirit, One God."

In the first three gospels, the record of Jesus' baptism is striking because it includes all three members of the Trinity at once:

> When all the people were being baptized, Jesus was baptized too. And as he was praying, heaven was opened and the Holy Spirit descended on him in bodily form like a dove. And a voice came from heaven:

"You are my Son, whom I love; with you I am well pleased." (Luke 3:21-22)

In choosing among the parallel gospel accounts, it is noteworthy that only Luke uses the expression "in bodily form" (or appearance) to describe how the Spirit descended (Luke 3:22). There are other significant differences.

The incarnation of Jesus adds to the mystery. Paul writes of God's unity, and relates it to the humanity of Christ: "There is one God, and one mediator between God and men, the man Christ Jesus" (1 Timothy 2:5). This important text is not an explanation of the Trinity. It is helpful because it declares God's unity and the specific role of Christ.

KEEP YOUR PERSPECTIVE

Remember that learning comes by approximation; it takes time to reduce the amount of error. It may be best to build up the idea first, then attach the technical term to it. You might point out what Christians do not believe about the Trinity. Be patient. A fully accurate statement about the doctrine of the Trinity is not necessary to salvation. The Bible emphasizes what must be believed about the Person of Christ.

Gently point out the arrogance of a position that denies revelation about God simply because it is incomprehensible to finite man. We view existence through our own experience; God's nature must not be limited by our ability to explain or understand Him.

The biblical concept of the Trinity is based on a vast number of passages. Allow time for God to instruct your friend. Theologians have worked hard to make the teaching precise. Keep sharpening your understanding with their help.

PRESENTING THE TRINITY

The process of communication will never be more severely tested than when you convey the idea of the Trinity to your Muslim friend. To say that words fail is a gross understatement. Be careful to speak the truth and avoid over-explanation. Never treat the three distinctions as three separate gods.

Personal relationships. The doctrine of the Trinity enables us to see how it is possible for God to have fellowship and express love within Himself from all eternity; He had no need of creatures in order to love. This should whet our appetites for more of Him. It was a North African, Augustine of Hippo (modern day Annaba, Algeria), who reminded the church of that practical reality.[3] Although it is not technically a *proof* of the Trinity, it is an important observation. As you read John's gospel, you will begin to find such qualities as obedience and humility within the Godhead—a startling, even shocking contrast to many of the Qur'anic terms that describe God. Check the terms *father* and *son* in your concordance for some exciting reading.

Illustrations. Diversity in the unity of the Creator is reflected in what He made and in human thought. To be sure, *all illustrations are inadequate,* but they do help us think. Humans think in picture language, and despite Muslim sensitivities, it is wise to follow the example of our Lord and use good pictures, appropriate to our listener, rather than to do without. Here are a few concrete suggestions:

- The one chemical substance of H_2O is always present in its three different forms—solid, liquid, and vapor.
- We experience a flame in its shape, its light, and its heat. (It is possible to see a certain analogy: the form suggests the supreme authority of the Father, the light the revealing role of the Son, the heat the invisible influence of the Spirit. The sun can also be used in this way.)

For more abstract thinkers, the following ideas might stimulate your thinking:

- To understand the world around us, we think in three dimensions. Space is one, but we know it in three dimensions.
- A tetrahedron is a solid with four identical faces. Each face is an equilateral triangle. The tetrahedron might be pressed

into service as an illustration. Notice that one, two, or three faces may be visible at the same time, while the fourth remains unseen. As creatures, we cannot know how much we do not know.

- We see the world of color in its infinite variety, using only three primary colors in our perception. (The weakness in this illustration is that the effect is really additive. The nice part is that we are seeing God in the rich color of His character when we discover the biblical teaching of the Trinity.)

Some people will take offense at the idea of any picture. Remember that illustrations are inadequate. They are often one-sided. Viewed alone, they can easily lead to a distortion of truth and doctrinal error. Do not be surprised that illustrations fail to convey the truth fully. But that is not to say they are useless. They are limited.

The foundation, the solid base of our belief that God is a Trinity, is in the teaching and pictures of the Bible itself. If your Muslim friends are willing, the best method of teaching the Trinity is simply to present the biblical basis of this great truth. Show them the actual Scripture passages. Ask your friend to sit alongside you; ask: "What does this mean to you? And this . . . ?"

FOR REFLECTION

1. What does it mean to a Muslim that God is merciful and compassionate? What does it mean to you?

2. Your Muslim friend says, "Yes, I know what you believe—God and Mary and Jesus and all that. I believe in Allah." If you could only make three brief points about the Trinity during a conversation, what would you want them to be?

3. How would you try to balance correction of misunderstandings on the one hand, and stimulation of interest for more information on the other hand?

4. Commit to memory some of the ancient creeds of the church as they touch on the doctrine of the Trinity.

CHAPTER ELEVEN

THE PERSON
OF JESUS

Who is Jesus? You will never stop learning the answer to this question, for it is part of the larger question of who God is. God has given us a beautiful and varied garden of stories, word pictures, and theological terms. Islam counters with its own array of alternatives, and the result is a garden that has its own dangerous beauties. The names and titles of our Lord are a great area for discussion, but first consider another fruitful starting point: the unique birth of Jesus.

THE BIRTH OF JESUS

Both the Qur'an and the Bible teach that Christ was born of a virgin (Qur'an 3:45-47):

> (And remember) when the angels said: O Mary! Lo! Allah giveth thee glad tidings of a word from Him, whose name is the Messiah, Jesus, son of Mary, illustrious in the world and in the Hereafter, and one of those brought near (unto Allah). He will speak unto mankind in his cradle and his manhood, and he is of the righteous. She said: My Lord! How can I have a child when no mortal hath touched me? He said: So (it will be). Allah createth what he will. If he decreeth a thing, He saith unto it only: Be! and it is.

Islam sees a different meaning in the virgin birth: Christ is like Adam; He is unique as a human being, but nothing more than a human being. Yet thinking about the virgin birth has helped some Muslims on the road to faith. Luke 1:26-38 and Matthew 1:18-25 give the biblical record.

You might consider this line of reasoning, which can help a thinking Muslim understand the true significance of the virgin birth:

> Adam was not born but created: Christ was born without a father. The creation of Adam was in this respect similar to the creation of the world, plants, and the lower animals; whereas the Qur'an itself says that Christ's supernatural birth took place through God's purpose to give men a sign, and this is not said of any other prophet's birth. To Abraham and Zacharias there was promised, according to the Qur'an, a "wise son," "a righteous prophet." But regarding Christ's birth the language used is very different, for of Mary it is said, "Her who kept her maidenhood, and into whom We breathed of Our spirit, and made her and her son a sign to all creatures" (Sura 21:91). The Qur'an therefore represents Christ's birth as without a parallel. The same language is used neither of Muhammad nor of anyone else. Why is this, except because Christ is superior to all other prophets?[1]

The Christian may well ask the Muslim why God chose to interrupt the natural course of events in this way. This could lead to studying New Testament passages (Romans 5:12-20; 1 Corinthians 15:20-50) that describe Jesus Christ as the *last Adam* and the *second man* and show how He has become the head of a new regenerated humanity. Regeneration was necessary because in *Adam* (i.e., generated from Him) all die, whereas *in Christ shall all be made alive.* God does nothing without reason; these passages explain His purpose in the virgin birth of Jesus.

There is an interesting lesson in our agreement that Jesus was born miraculously, of a virgin: the *meaning* of the miracle is as important as the *fact* of the miracle. So, too, agreement about other crucial facts, such as Jesus' death, is not enough. Both the fact and its meaning are important.

NAMES AND TITLES OF JESUS

Both the Qur'an and the Bible refer to Jesus in language that is not used of any other person. Muslims and Christians use these names to explain their belief. First, we turn to the Qur'an. It is worth reading the whole quotation to get the Qur'anic picture attached to the word.

NAMES AND TITLES OF JESUS IN THE QUR'AN

Christ. In Arabic, the form of the word *MasiiH* suggests the meaning "anointed," but most Muslims understand it as a personal name rather than a title.

> When the angels said: O Mary! Lo! Allah giveth thee glad tidings of a word from Him, whose name is the Messiah, Jesus, son of Mary, illustrious in the world and in the Hereafter, and one of those brought near (unto Allah). (Qur'an 3:45)

Jesus. The Arabic name (*'Isa*) was probably formed by modification to rhyme with Moses (*Musa*).[2] There has been considerable controversy among Christians about whether this name should be used in Arabic translations of the Bible or in evangelizing Muslims. The traditional Christian Arabic name for Jesus is *Yasuu'*. It is worth observing that *'Isa* is the standard name for Jesus among some non-Arabic Christian minorities who live in Muslim societies.

> Say (O Muhammad): We believe in Allah and that which is revealed unto us and that which was revealed unto Abraham and Ishamel and Isaac and Jacob and the tribes, that that which was vouchsafed unto Moses and Jesus and the Prophets from their Lord. We make no distinction between any of them, and unto Him we have surrendered. (Qur'an 3:84)

Son of Mary. This name is used frequently and contains an implied contrast with the Christian title *Son of God.*

> And We gave unto Jesus, son of Mary, clear proofs (of Allah's sovereignty), and We supported him with the holy Spirit. (Qur'an 2:87)

A Word from God; His Word. In reading the texts that follow, you may feel that there are still some traces of Christian belief remaining in the terms, although a number of Muslim interpreters would like to prove you wrong. Christians often have used the idea of God's Word in speaking to Muslims. For example, "Do you understand this name [*kalimat allah*] of *al-masiiH* [Christ]? My word comes from my very being. In saying this of Christ, it [the Bible] means that He is divine, uniquely God's Son."

In Qur'an 3:39, Zachariah, the father of John the Baptist, hears the promise of John's birth. John will confirm "a word from God":

> And the angels called to him as he stood praying in the sanctuary: Allah giveth thee good tidings of (a son whose name is) John, (who cometh) to confirm a word from Allah, lordly, chaste, a Prophet of the righteous.

In another place, Jesus is "His word" (*kalimatuhu*). This passage also refers to Jesus as a "spirit from God" and a "messenger of God."

> O People of the Scripture! Do not exaggerate in your religion nor utter aught concerning Allah save the truth. The Messiah, Jesus son of Mary, was only a messenger of Allah, and His word which He conveyed unto Mary, and a spirit from Him. So believe in Allah and His messengers, and say not "Three"—Cease! (it is) better for you!—Allah is only One God. Far is it removed from His transcendant majesty that he should have a son. His is all that is in the heavens and all that is in the earth. And Allah is sufficient as Defender. (Qur'an 4:171)

Other titles. Qur'an 19:30 identifies Jesus as a "Prophet" and tells the story of the birth of Jesus, who speaks while still in the cradle:

> He spake: Lo! I am the slave of Allah. He hath given me the Scripture and hath appointed me a Prophet.

Jesus is given an exalted position in the Qur'an, called "Illustrious in this World and the Next." Consider Qur'an 3:45:

(And remember) when the angels said: O Mary! Lo! Allah giveth thee glad tidings of a word from Him, whose name is the Messiah, Jesus, son of Mary, illustrious in the world and in the Hereafter, and one of those brought near (unto Allah).

The Qur'an really does give Jesus a high place, so high at times that it is not surprising that the grace of God has used these terms to lead people beyond the Qur'an. But keep things in perspective by remembering that titles are used lavishly in Islam. Compare the descriptions of Jesus with those attributed to Muhammed.

MUHAMMED AND HIS TITLES

After his death, Muhammed became an object of increasing veneration. He is viewed as the perfect man; all that he did is considered revelatory. In some sects of Islam, Muhammed's praise expands to occupy a large area of devotional life. The following words describing Muhammed were gleaned from a Muslim devotional text in which the Muslim asks God to bless the prophet:

> The sea of Thy lights, the mine of Thy secrets, the tongue of Thy plea, the bridegroom of Thy kingdom . . . the seal of Thy prophets. . . . our lord and master [often] . . . who lightens the darkness. . . . the bringer of mercy. . . . the lord of the Pool to which the people will come to drink. . . the intercessor . . . the lord of mediation. . . . the way of access. . . . the lord of virtue. . . . the possessor of the staff . . . the possessor of the convincing proof. . . . who has the crown. . . . who will be the intercessor for all men. . . . the bringer of good tidings . . . the bright-shining lamp . . . the pure one . . . the one who is sweet and perfumed . . . from whose light all lights have come forth.[3]

To be sure, many Muslims would reject this kind of thing. But some treasure it. You should remember that a devotional vacuum represents a genuine need, and as a vacuum it will seek filling. In speaking of Christ, it is a mistake to engage in a contest of religious one-upmanship. That is all too familiar to Muslims.

NAMES AND TITLES OF JESUS IN THE BIBLE

There are so many rich expressions in the Bible that you must turn to reference books for an adequate treatment. But two terms have special importance for Muslims: *Son of God* and *Word of God.* Muslims are conditioned to think that what is divine cannot also be human, and what is human cannot also be divine. If Jesus was a man, He was not God in any sense. First Timothy 2:5 is helpful at the meeting of human and divine:

> For there is one God and one mediator between God and men, the man Christ Jesus, who gave himself as a ransom for all men.

The Word became flesh. So it is important to include the human part (e.g., *Son of Man*) when you talk of Jesus. Otherwise Muslims may think that you are trying to prove that Jesus was God without being man.[4]

Jesus the Son of God. The Bible reveals our Lord Jesus as the eternal Son of God who appeared in human flesh. The term *Son of God* is one of the greatest hurdles for a Muslim to overcome in understanding and accepting the biblical picture of Jesus. The term packs a strong emotional message for most Muslims, like a disgusting insult to God Most High. Here is how one ordinary Muslim explains the Father-Son relationship:

> First of all, what is the meaning of "Father"? "Father" means that he married and sired children. And marriage is an animal function. And you claim that God is "the Father." So God is an animal?! That's not logical . . . ! Did He tell you that?[5]

Iskander Jadeed quotes the Qur'an, then the famous commentator Al Baidawi, and concludes that "there is no sonship in Qur'anic thinking save reproductive (sexual) sonship."[6]

Before you can get to the true biblical teaching, you must try to disarm the misunderstanding. At this point many Christians are happy to accept at face value what is said in one of the best known and most often repeated portions, Qur'an 112. If you are learning Arabic, it is well worth knowing this sura by heart.

> Say: He is Allah, the One! Allah, the eternally Besought of all! He be-
> getteth not nor was begotten. And there is none comparable unto Him.

A Christian agreeing with this would explain that the *eternal generation* of the Son refers to an *eternal relationship,* not to an event by which the Son was created. The biblical teaching is utterly removed from what many people think we believe. Christians have never believed Jesus to be the Son of God in a physical sense.[7] The term *Ibn* (Son) is often used in a metaphorical sense as well as a physical one. Helping Muslims understand the *spiritual* sense in which you use the term will often enable a sincere Muslim to overcome this hurdle. It is usually much better to say *spiritual* than *metaphorical.*

When you teach the meaning of the biblical term *Son of God,* do not try to pour the full theological meaning into every occurrence. The expression does not always have the eternality of the Son in view. Sometimes it tells of His high and glorious position, and His closeness to God. The greatest emphasis on the eternity of the Son comes in the fourth gospel; John leads us to the Son of God by speaking of the eternal Word.

Jesus the Word of God. One of the most profound works of literature for Muslims compares the terms *Word of God* and *Son of God* in this way:

> The fact should be noted that, when philosophical language is used in the Gospel, our Lord Jesus Christ is styled "the Word of God" (kalimatullah), as in John 1:1. The other title, Son of God (ibnullah), has really the same meaning, but it is used for two special reasons: (1) for the benefit of simple people, who are the great majority of the human race, and who would not understand the former phrase, and (2) because it enables us to realize the personality of the Word of God (kalimatullah) and the love which exists between the Divine Hypostases [Persons] of the Holy Trinity (compare John 15:9, 10; 17:23, 26). Neither of these latter facts could be expressed by the title "the Word of God." It is true that no human vocables can be well suited to express at all fully and correctly the realities of the Divine Nature, but we cannot be wrong in employing the terms used in the Holy Scriptures by men who wrote under Divine Guidance and Inspiration.[8]

THE INCARNATION

In speaking of Christ as God the Son, Christians are never far from the mysteries of the incarnation. Meditation on the prologue to the Gospel of John (1:1-18), with the help of study aids, is essential. The opening verses are prime candidates for memorization, whether you are in contact with traditional or modernized Muslims. If you are learning Arabic, consider memorizing *al-Kalima* (just seven verses), the opening chapter of *The Life of the Messiah in a Classical Arabic Tongue,* for your own needs as well as those of others.

The eternal perspective also comes out in the phrase, "He appeared in a body" (1 Timothy 3:16). To counter the impression that small size or material life is a defect, it may help to speak in terms of God's *ability* to take on human nature as the perfect way of revealing Himself and saving mankind. It is the power of God expressing His love, taking the form of weakness.

FOR REFLECTION

1. Review the birth and childhood narratives pertaining to Jesus in the Qur'an and the Bible. What impressions do you gain from comparing the two? Note the similarities and divergences.
2. What words can you use to express the biblical idea of the sonship of Christ? What problem areas in communication need special attention?
3. Examine the titles of Jesus that appear both in the Qur'an and in the Bible. Are the meanings identical? What titles would you emphasize in talking with your friends?
4. What belief about Jesus is necessary for salvation? How can you convey that to your Muslim friend? Is it possible for a Muslim to be saved without acknowledging the deity of Jesus? Defend your answer from Scripture.

CHAPTER TWELVE

THE DEATH
OF JESUS

In the incarnation and the cross, we are at the heart of the difference between Islam and Christianity. Here, revelation helps us to answer the question, "What is God really like?"

ISLAM AND THE DEATH OF JESUS

Did Jesus really die on the cross? Some Muslims acknowledge His death, but the overwhelming majority deny it.[1] The Qur'an is not entirely clear. But there can be no doubt that almost all Muslims *understand* the Qur'an to teach that Jesus did not die, and that Qur'anic references to Jesus' death mean that He will die in the future. Here are a few key Qur'anic texts:

> Peace be upon me the day I was born, and the day I die, and the day I shall be raised alive! (Qur'an 19:33)

> And they (the disbelievers) schemed, and Allah schemed (against them): and Allah is the best of schemers. (And remember) when Allah said: O Jesus! Lo! I am gathering[2] thee and causing thee to ascend unto me, and am cleansing thee of those who disbelieved and am setting those who follow thee above those who disbelieved until the Day of Resurrection. Then unto Me ye will (all) return, and I shall judge between you as to that wherein ye used to differ. (Qur'an 3:54-55)

And because of their saying: We slew the Messiah Jesus son of Mary, Allah's messenger—they slew him not nor crucified, but it appeared so unto them; and lo! those who disagree concerning it are in doubt thereof; they have no knowledge thereof save pursuit of a conjecture; they slew him not for certain, but Allah took him up unto Himself. Allah was ever Mighty, Wise. (Qur'an 4:157-58)

To the Muslim it is unthinkable that God should allow His holy prophet to die on a cross. Such a death is seen as the epitome of defeat and failure, whereas escape from death is seen as the sign of God's triumphant intervention. Here is a yawning chasm of misunderstanding between Islam and Christianity:

- **Christ,** when He was faced with opposition by the authorities, desertion by His friends, and the hostility of the crowds, "resolutely set out for Jerusalem" (Luke 9:51). He knew He would soon face torture and death.

- **Muhammed,** when faced with opposition by the authorities in Mecca and desertion by almost all of his family, fled to Medina. Notice the crucial difference. Muhammed went through battles and difficulty, but he finally *avoided* an early and violent death, and prospered. To Muslims, this was God's vindication of His prophet.

- But **Christ triumphed over death** by going through death itself. As Muslims grasp this wonderful fact, they can at last understand the significance of the cross and see it as a sign of victory and a subject of praise.

WHAT DOES THE CROSS MEAN TO A MUSLIM?

In the Crusades, great numbers of "Christians" abandoned the way of the cross, while holding the symbol so high that the Crusades are known in Arabic as the "Cross Wars." Historians tell of needless slaughter by Christians and generosity on the part of their Muslim adversaries. The cross became the symbol of a religion that was hostile, foreign, and cruel. You can understand why wars of European colonial expansion and the establishment of Israel (and the suffering of Palestinians), with "Christian" support, seem like an extension of the Crusades. Jesus will return, Muslims believe—but when He does, He will break all the crosses.

OVERCOMING THE OFFENSE OF THE CROSS

How can you help your Muslim friend accept the fact and the significance of Christ's death and resurrection? It is worth reminding yourself that the answer depends on the nature of the obstacle.

> The God of this age has blinded the minds of unbelievers, so that they cannot see the light of the gospel of the glory of Christ, who is the image of God. (2 Corinthians 4:4)

The whole of 2 Corinthians 4 is worth repeated meditation. As you look around, you can see blinding in individual hearts. The outer world of culture (your own and others) is enemy territory where we are called to do battle. Meditate on Ephesians 2:2 and 2 Corinthians 10:5. Our first duty and constant resource is prayer.

DO NOT SEPARATE THE CROSS FROM THE REST OF THE GOOD NEWS

The gospel is about a series of closely related truths: the incarnation, the crucifixion, the resurrection, the ascension, our Lord's present ministry of intercession, and the expectation of His return. This linking can be observed as a dominant theme in the apostolic preaching in Acts and in the gospel's summary definition in 1 Corinthians 15. When the cross is isolated from these other events, its importance is skewed and the event is misunderstood.

STRESS THE POSITIVE EFFECTS OF THE CROSS

The gospel means victory over sin, Satan, and death. The cross was a spiritual battle in which Christ experienced the full power of death and then rose in victory, bringing a whole new creation along with Him. It was a display of God's glory, power, and sovereignty. Notice how the New Testament emphasizes fulfilled prophecy, which stands in stark contrast to the common idea that the cross portrays God's inability to rescue Jesus. Here is the power of redemption, and redemption is a positive word among Muslims.

USE GRAPHIC ILLUSTRATIONS OF THE TRUTH

The rich treasures of the Bible, of Arab Muslim history and culture, and of nature can help to bring home the message of redemption in all of its warmth, color, and excitement.

- Use Bible stories such as that of Abraham, Isaac, and the sacrifice in Genesis 22. Most Muslims believe it was Ishmael, not Isaac, who was about to be sacrificed. It is best to avoid that controversy, at least until your friend has read the biblical story.
- Ask what your Muslim friends believe about the sacrifices in their own traditions.
- The Qur'an has bridges to the biblical idea of redemption. You can refer to the Qu'ran, or use the words to good effect. Here is a sample: the Qur'an tells the story of Genesis 22; after God calls to Abraham that he need not sacrifice his son, the story continues: "Then we ransomed him with a tremendous victim" (Qur'an 37:107). What was this mighty sacrifice? Just one ram? Is it the yearly sacrifice of the pilgrims at Mecca? If not, what?
- God's creation contains many living illustrations of sacrifice for others and life after death. Jesus chose a perfect example in the death of the seed, the life of the plant, and the fruit that results. Notice the same kind of thing in the change of the seasons (winter to spring in temperate climates, alternation between green and dry in much of the Arab world). Many animals are moved by instinct to defend their young, or their group, at the cost of their lives.

DEMONSTRATE THE PURPOSE OF CHRIST'S DEATH

Proclaim God's purpose in the sacrifice (John 10:17-18). It includes the wise eternal counsel of God, in contrast to the idea that God was surprised by the unfolding of events. Old Testament prophecy shows that the death of Christ is built into the message of the Bible from beginning to end. Christ had to die because God is both loving and just in all He does. Your Muslim friend needs to know what you believe about this and how you feel about it. The cross speaks powerfully to the problem of evil and human experience of suffering.

PRESENT THE GOSPEL ACCOUNT

The four gospels cover the events of the crucifixion in greater detail than any other portion of Jesus' life. The details are so abundant and consistent that it is impossible to set aside the crucifixion accounts. John devotes nearly half of his gospel to the crucifixion and events that immediately precede it. The reality of Christ's death is evident from Matthew 27:33-50, Mark 15:43-47, and John 19:32-37. It would be impossible for the disciples (not to mention His own mother), who were present and who buried the body, to mistake Him for someone else. The wounds were clearly visible in the risen Christ (John 20:27). The narratives are packed with reference to fulfilled prophecy, showing that God was in control and that Christ was deliberately offering His life for humanity. You may add that the fact of Christ's death is substantiated by non-Christian historians. Remember that it is not the word *cross* that is important, especially at first, but the biblical teaching. It is a record of God's love and victory.

LIVE THE CROSS

If you think back to the people whom God used to leave a deep and lasting impression on your life, it is likely that you saw them living the reality of being "crucified with Christ" (Galatians 2:20). You came to understand what they were doing—what it cost them, why they did it. Someone prayed. God worked. Now it is your turn to live sacrificially before your Muslim friends.

FOR REFLECTION

1. Your Muslim friend returns a Gospel, saying "I liked the part about Jesus teaching and healing people." After talking a bit more, you recognize that your friend really did read most of the

book but does not want to talk about the death of Christ. You decide to risk raising the subject anyway. How will you introduce the subject? If your friend agrees to continue the discussion, what will you say?

2. Meditate on 1 Corinthians 15:3-8. What are the great events in the life of Jesus that define the good news? How does Paul tie them together in the context?

3. What does it mean to depend upon (have faith in, trust) the sacrifice of Christ? What difference does that make to you? To your Muslim friend?

4. What principles underlie the ability to give true and persuasive Christian answers to Muslim misunderstandings of the gospel?

CHAPTER THIRTEEN

A PERSPECTIVE ON MUHAMMED

You want to know what your Muslim friends think of Jesus, so it is no surprise that they want to know what you think of Muhammed. This can be a very sensitive subject. Approach the issue after careful reflection and prayer.

Christians have taken many different positions concerning Muhammed. Some see him as a demonically inspired antichrist. Others attempt to balance the positive and negative effects of his life. Still others have warmly accepting views that try to squeeze in some sort of prophethood. Recognize that you may feel one way about Muhammed as a *person* and another way about his claim to be a *prophet.*

All Muslims believe that Muhammed is the apostle of God, thus accepting the authority of the Qur'an. But Muslims have many different ways of thinking about Muhammed. The Muhammed of the Qur'an (and some traditions) holds a high place, but it is not the place of the idealized, perfect man created over time by the growth of tradition and devotional practice. Tradition is based on the principle that every word and act of Muhammed was revelatory. You need to remember that God truly has provided a perfect Man who can be the object of devotion. Islam's creation of a substitute, after the death of Muhammed, reflects the hidden hunger that Christ alone can satisfy.

If the issue is so sensitive, and Muhammed means different things to different Muslims, how should you answer? If the full authority of the Bible is our starting point, it is inconsistent to accept the apostleship of Muhammed. In general, it is wise not to attack Muhammed; but some believe that, in reality, Muhammed is the Achilles' heel of Islam. You might consider gently sowing the seeds of a healthy doubt by asking questions (e.g., "Would you recommend that a fifty-year-old-man marry a girl of twelve?"). This obviously requires some study of the life of Muhammed. Another suggestion is to ask why Muslims pray for Muhammed.

Do not forget the personal side of the issue. Many Muslims believe that Muhammed was a supremely virtuous man, and they are deeply attached to him. Your friend's question about how you feel about Muhammed may also mean "How do you feel about me and my ideals?"

DOES THE BIBLE CONTAIN PROPHECIES OF MUHAMMED?

If Muhammed really were the successor of Moses, David, and Jesus, it would be natural to expect that their books would contain prophecy pointing forward to him. The Qur'an itself expresses this expectation; God speaks to Moses:

> Those who believe Our revelations; Those who follow the messenger, the Prophet who can neither read nor write, whom they will find described in the Torah and the Gospel (which are) with them. (Qur'an 7:156-57)

The "Prophet who can neither read nor write" is, of course, Muhammed. Muslims may appeal to Deuteronomy 18:18 as a biblical reflection of this same divine promise:

> I will raise up for them a prophet like you [Moses] from among their brothers; I will put my words in his mouth, and he will tell them everything I command him.

Muslims also take references to the Paraclete (John 14:16-17, 25-26; 16:7-11) as predictions about Muhammed. This interpretive understanding follows Qur'an 61:6.

And when Jesus son of Mary said: O Children of Israel! Lo! I am the messenger of Allah unto you, confirming that which was (revealed) before me in the Torah, and bringing good tidings of a messenger who cometh after me, whose name is the Praised One. Yet when he hath come unto them with clear proofs, they say: This is mere magic.

Muslim interpreters say that "The Praised One" (*Ahmad,* an equivalent of Muhammed) refers to an original Greek word that was later corrupted to the reading *paracletos.* But this is pure speculation and flies in the face of reasonable expectation.[1] Some Muslims claim that many other passages predict Muhammed's coming, and they suppose that still more predictions have been removed from the Bible. Claims such as these often serve only to divert attention from the true spiritual issues. But when Muslims are willing to give time to careful Bible study, it can be an open door.

DOES MUHAMMED MEET BIBLICAL CRITERIA FOR PROPHETS?

The key passage is Deuteronomy 18:15-22; it should be studied in light of Deuteronomy 13:1-5 and 34:10-12. Note the element of predictive prophecy, verification, and miracles. These passages are part of a larger body of Old Testament material on prophets and prophecy. In the Gospels, there is the expectation of Elijah and the Messiah, with no one of comparable stature expected after the Messiah. Jesus warns solemnly against deception by false prophets. Emphasize that throughout the Bible, the message of a prophet must be consistent with previous revelation. The warning of Deuteronomy 13 is repeated in 1 John 4:1-6 and illustrated by the false prophet of Revelation.

The contrast between the claims of Christ and Muhammed may not be lost on your Muslim friend. After patient reflection,

a learned Maulavi from Swat, now a Christian convert, was first brought to doubt Muhammad's claims by reflecting upon the du'aa or petition, in which, at the close of the fixed prayers (salawat), a Muslim says, "O Lord, have mercy upon and give peace to Muhammed," etc. The thought arose in his mind, "In no other religion is it thought necessary to pray for God's mercy on its founder. Why then is Muhammed prayed for?" He next noticed that in the kalimah or Muhammadan creed the title given to Muhammad is merely rasul, or "apostle"; he is not even called a nabi or "prophet," whereas far higher titles are given to Christ in the Qur'an itself. In argument it would be well to put these objections to Muhammad's claims either in the form of the tale told here, or as questions, asking, e.g., "Why is it necessary for Muslims to pray for Muhammed?" This leads the inquirer to form his own conclusions.[2]

FOR REFLECTION

1. "Muhammed came preaching that people should believe in Allah, repent of their sins, and do good works. He wonderfully transformed his own society and united many diverse tribes and peoples in a brotherhood where all races are equal. Why don't you accept Muhammed as a prophet of God like those who preceded him?" How would you reply?

2. What positive things can you say about the life and influence of Muhammed?

Part 3
Strategies for Ministry

CHAPTER FOURTEEN

COMMUNICATING THE GOSPEL

Faith, prayer, love for God, the fruit of the Spirit, Christ's presence and power. These spiritual factors provide the energy for evangelism. But energy must be channeled to be effective. The development of these channels involves matters of strategy, such as deciding what to say and how to say it. This chapter takes a look at some of those questions.

THE GOSPEL AND ISLAM

As you set out to communicate the gospel to your Muslim friend you immediately find the imposing edifice of Islamic teaching. You must decide what you are going to do about Islam. There are three basic options: knock the edifice down, build upon it, or walk around it.

The *knock it down* approach involves using evidence and arguments to show Islam's weaknesses and the gospel's superiority. This does not need to be done in an unfriendly, disrespectful way, although it may result in great personal discomfort. Many Christians adopt the *knock it down* stance at least occasionally, and some publications focus on it. If you decide not to use this strategy a certain amount of determination will be required. Many Muslims have adopted this approach regarding the Christian faith, so they are quick to bring out their own arguments, and it is natural to want to counterattack. This polemic approach frequently results in a broken friendship; remember that for most Muslims, religious conviction is a matter of faith and culture. These are not often changed by argumentation.

The *build upon it* strategy aims at using what is good in Islam, such as Qur'anic verses that support the Bible, to convince Muslims of the truth of Christ. Some very creative applications of this approach have been developed in recent years. One of the dangers of this strategy may be an implied endorsement of certain aspects of Islam.

The *walk around it* option assumes that the best way to get the central gospel story before the eyes and into the heart of Muslims is to present it directly and positively, avoiding possible complications arising from heavy interaction with Islamic teaching. This way of proceeding has several strong features. Many have found it particularly appropriate in personal conversations where the Christian is from Europe or North America and the Muslim from the Middle East. Everything that follows in this chapter is based on the *walk around it* approach.

Whichever approach you adopt in your conversations, be aware of what method you are using and evaluate the practical implications of your choice.

UNDERSTAND ISLAM

Deciding to *walk around Islam* is not the same thing as ignoring it. On the contrary, it is important to know all you can about Islam. Pay attention to Islam's *language*. Words such as *sin* and *prayer,* for instance, which are so important to Christians, are also important in Islamic teaching, but with differences in meaning. You must also be aware of Islam's *concepts*. Running through the gospel are definite ideas concerning such things as the character of God and the nature of humanity. Islamic understanding of these and other matters is not the same as that of Christianity, so extra care is required for clear communication to take place. It is good to know points of agreement, and even more vital to know where points of conflict lie. For example, the assertion that Jesus is the Son of God often produces a negative reaction. Blundering into the subject can hinder the progress of your conversations. But if you know this is a difficult area, you can carefully prepare how and when you want to talk about Christ's sonship.

UNDERSTAND MUSLIMS

Understanding Islam is one thing, understanding the Muslim sitting in front of you is another. Expertise in Islam may tell you that, according to Islamic teaching, it is easy for God to forgive sin, and guilt is not a major problem. Your friend, however, may have tremendous guilt from not following all of Islam's teachings, especially in comparison with members of Muslim fundamentalist groups in town. Your knowledge of Islam may enable you to co-gently argue against the assertion that the coming of Muhammed was predicted by Jesus. But acquaintance with Muslims warns you that your friend will never let you win this kind of argument.

Individuals of Muslim background vary as much as individuals of Christian background. Characteristics change from country to country. You must get to know your Muslim friend.

KEEP YOUR EYE ON THE GOSPEL

Guard your conversation. It can be very easy to talk religion with a Muslim. If you do not bring up the subject, perhaps your friend will. But this is not always a sign that you are making progress. How much should you talk about Christ, the Bible, or Christianity? As much as you can? Maybe not.

Guard against developing an adversarial relationship. Conversation can easily degenerate to "your ideas against my ideas, your religion against my religion, your people against mine, your culture against mine." If this happens, your friend will have a strong emotional need to prove you wrong. You want to present Christ to your friend. Insofar as you represent Western culture and thought, keep yourself out of the way. As a friend and follower of Jesus, the more your friend sees and hears of you the better. Become a model of Ephesians 4:25–5:2 and 1 Thessalonians 2:7-13.

It is possible to devote time to side issues that are close to the gospel but are really not part of the life-giving message. It takes great concentration and effort to stick to the essentials of the gospel. You might discuss the reliability of the Bible, for instance, or show that Jesus did not really predict the coming of Muhammed. But these things are not at the heart of the gospel story.

You may think that these issues lay a foundation for the message, but do not be too quick to assume that is the case. For example, consider the issue of the gospel's reliability. Must your friend believe as you do in order to understand the Scripture's message? A better approach is simply to study a key passage about Jesus and let the gospel speak for itself.

KEEP YOUR EYE ON THE PERSON

As you concentrate on the story of Christ, do your best to see that the message finds its way to the heart and mind of your friend. There are many things that can stand in the way. Be alert for two dangers in particular.

- *Discussion of central gospel truth that never penetrates beyond a superficial level.* You may discuss a key point at length (e.g., the necessity of the atonement) without your friend really understanding its significance or allowing it to touch the inner person.
- *Movement at the feeling level from a receptive attitude to a rejecting one.* Become sensitive to early warning signs of this change in mood. When you sense it developing, back away from provocation. Return to the issue on another day. If you press on, your friend's emotions can crystallize into permanent rejection. Suppose that you are studying the Bible together. Your friend raises an objection to something in the reading. You respond. The Muslim restates the objection. The more your friend says, the higher the emotional content becomes. It may not have been a key issue in the first place, but it has grown to dominate your friend's thinking.

It may help to think of your friend as an open door that can be easily closed and locked. Your friend is at ease with familiar ideas. You come knocking at the door, bringing a suspicious-looking stranger, the message of Christ. Your friend slowly opens the door and lets you in, but remains uncertain and insecure about the stranger you have brought along. You introduce your friend to Jesus, developing an acquaintance with His character. Don't worry if your friend cannot accept or understand everything the first time. A few clear, positive, firsthand impressions will be enough. The important thing is to leave the door open for a second encounter.

READ THE GOSPELS

Give your friend one of the four Gospels to read. Do this when a religious issue is raised. You might say something like, "If you are interested in knowing more about this, the best thing is to read for yourself what Jesus said and did. Here, I'll loan you a Gospel." The Gospel of Luke is a good choice, or perhaps Mark.

The Gospels present Jesus very attractively and persuasively, since the writers wanted to attract people to Jesus. You want your friend's first contact with Christianity to create a thirst for more. The Gospels can awaken that desire in a Muslim.

☐ An Iraqi student asked her Christian classmate for a copy of *her book*. She took the New Testament and began to read avidly, especially the Gospels. She came to her classmate every day with new questions about what she had read. Not the *I have an objection* kind of questions, but those that say *I want to understand*. In class she could be seen ignoring the lesson and reading the New Testament. This went on for about three weeks until, unexpectedly, she returned to Iraq. The ending of her story is not known, but at least she was off to a running start.

BEGIN WITH JESUS

There is much to be said for an evangelistic presentation that begins and ends with Jesus Christ. Why save the best for last? The heart of the good news lies in the activity of Jesus; the final choice centers on Him. It is Jesus, the living Person portrayed in the gospel accounts, who can best gain an initial positive response from Muslims. But many prefer to begin with the Old Testament when presenting the gospel to Muslims. There are two good reasons for doing so. First, it is possible to take advantage of common ground by beginning with prophets already known to Muslims: among them Adam, Noah, Abraham, and Moses. Second, the gospel will be firmly set in the context of monotheism, with the nature and character of God clearly set forth.

ENCOURAGE BIBLE STUDY

An action step can be a key to get the message of Christ through to your Muslim friend. Offer to get together for a few Bible reading sessions. If your friend accepts the suggestion, you can go on to say, "There may be things you don't understand the first time you read the gospel of Luke. If you would like I can explain a few basic things to help you get the overall picture of what it is about." Your role is not to tell your friend everything, but to encourage reading, study, and discovery with understanding. Do not try to prove that it is true; explain what the Bible is saying.

Plan a set time with your friend that is specifically devoted to this purpose. Carefully select your passages beforehand. Focus on one main, straightforward idea during each time together. Remember to limit the time as mentioned earlier. Don't try to cover the whole story in one session. Detailed suggestions are included in chapter 17.

FOCUS ON CONCRETE IDEAS

A big part of the Gospels' power lies in the concreteness of their presentation of Jesus. They are full of little details about Him: His words, His activities, His attitudes, His responses to various situations and people. Each detail has an impact. Like the original disciples, the reader progressively gets to know Jesus. Also like the disciples, the reader must wait for answers to every question. But when the great theological affirmations about Christ finally come, your Muslim friend is better prepared to receive them.

You may be tempted to bypass the concrete detail of the gospel narratives, going immediately into a systematic doctrinal presentation of the plan of salvation, including such elements as human need, God's provision, and Jesus as God and man. You may want to go directly to the more doctrinal portions of Scripture. Save them for later examination.

☐ Consider the experience of a group of Christians camping on a beach in North Africa. They got to know a group of Muslims who were also camping. After a few days, one of the Christians set a time with a young schoolteacher to show him some things in the Bible. As the time drew near the Christian was not sure what passage to choose. Finally he decided to tackle the hard issues head-on and go directly to the core of it all: the incarnation presented in the first chapter of John's gospel. The study did not work. It became hopelessly bogged down. Analyzing what went wrong, the Christian saw that much of the problem stemmed from beginning with such a difficult issue. It was not only the issue that caused problems, but the way in which the issue was introduced. With no preparation and almost no knowledge of the personality and activities of Jesus, the Muslim was confronted with statements asserting that Jesus was with God and was God. To him, Jesus was just a name, empty of meaning.

Too much new information was given all at once, and it was packaged in an abstract form. The problem was that the Muslim schoolteacher could not absorb it all. A few simple ideas communicated through the concrete images of Jesus' deeds, parables, and conversations might have created more of a thirst.

AIM FOR THE HEART

When selecting texts to read, choose passages that appeal to the heart. It is difficult to break through from a theoretical or historical discussion to a deeper level where the inner person is really affected. Actually, most of the Bible tends to touch the heart of a person. But look for passages that exhibit this response-inviting quality to a high degree: passages where love is shown, needs are met, demands are made. For example: the parable of the prodigal son, the Pharisee and the sinner praying in the Temple, the sinful woman whose tears fell on Jesus' feet, or Jesus' warning about gaining the world and losing the soul.

FOR REFLECTION

1. What are the strengths and weaknesses of the three options for dealing with Islam? Can you conceive of situations where each might be advantageous?
2. What is the gospel? Can you state it clearly in one or two complete sentences?
3. What issues do we associate with the good news that are really not essential to understanding and receiving the gospel?
4. Choose four or five incidents from the Gospels. Assess the emotional impact of Jesus' words on his listeners? What emotional and behavioral impact might these stories have for your friend?

CHAPTER FIFTEEN

APPROACHING PROBLEM AREAS

There are a number of issues you should avoid or approach with caution. Some involve misconceptions that are problematic to a Muslim's clear understanding of the good news. Others are not foundational to the gospel, and addressing them will only distract from the message.

EXPRESSING YOUR OPINION OF ISLAM

Try not to be critical of Islam. Criticizing your friend's belief will cut off a hearing for the gospel. Listen to what your friend says about Islam; if asked for your opinion, you may want to say, "What I really know about is Jesus and the Bible. I can't really say too much about Islam." It is quite possible that when you propose a Bible reading session your friend will say "OK. I will read the Bible with you if you study the Qur'an with me." Take your friend up on this offer. It will enable you to move toward the message of Christ, and you will learn more about your friend's thinking.

ISSUES OF DEBATE BETWEEN MUSLIMS AND CHRISTIANS

Avoid issues of debate between Muslims and Christians. Some of these will be resolved as a Muslim responds favorably to other parts of the gospel story. Some hard issues must be addressed, but they are better left until your friend has a generally positive attitude toward Christ. When a person is looking for something to protest, discussion of the hard points is generally a waste of effort.

☐ A university student in North Africa went through a series of gospel reading sessions and responded very positively to Jesus and the Bible. He knew Christians believed that Jesus was God's Son and equal with God; at several points he asked about this. But, apart from explaining that *Son of God* did not mean a physical relationship, his Christian friend suggested that they wait to get into that topic. When they finally looked at what the Bible said about Christ's deity, the student could not accept it. For several weeks he was caught at this point. He told his Christian friend: "If you had tried to tell me all this at the beginning I would have rejected it with no hesitation. But now I am stuck. I can't accept that Jesus is one with God; but I can't reject it either, because now I believe everything else the Bible says about Jesus." After a time he fully accepted the Bible's teaching about Christ's relationship to God.

THE CRUCIFIXION OF JESUS

Jesus' death on the cross is a trouble spot because it directly contradicts Muslim belief. But if your friend responds favorably to one or two gospel reading sessions, it is a subject you can examine early in your discussions. It is fundamental to genuine belief and will immediately confront anyone who reads the Gospels. Spend one session just on the fact of the cross, leaving consideration of its meaning until another time. You might approach the subject by looking at the predictions Jesus made about His death. They show that Jesus' death was no mistake or surprise. Consider Mark 8:27-33, where Peter gives a preview of a common Muslim objection to the cross and Jesus makes a strong reply.

THE NECESSITY FOR ATONEMENT

Atonement is a key subject because the standard Islamic conception of sin and of God sees no need for atonement. It is best to present a few simple images (e.g., the sacrificial lamb) that communicate the point forcefully than to begin a comprehensive study of passages that deal with the abstract idea. Isaiah 53 is a good passage to read together. Emphasize the fact that it was written centuries before the time of Jesus, and that several verses speak of the significance of Christ's death for us personally: our gifts, our sorrows, our crimes, our sins, our well-being, our healing. Romans 5:6-8 and 8:31-39 are also powerfully attractive and appeal to the heart.

THE DEITY OF CHRIST

Defer discussion about the nature of Christ until your friend believes, or is inclined to believe, what has already been read in the Bible. Speak with confidence when you look at passages that speak of Christ's unity with God. Do not justify, defend, or make easy the doctrine of Christ's deity. Make this simple point: this is what the Bible teaches. If you accept the Bible's reliability, you accept that Jesus is one with God. You build on your friend's previously established confidence in what the Bible says about Christ.

Remind your friend that the Bible consistently teaches that there is only one God; read Mark 12:29-30 together. This conviction forms the essential background to what you say about Christ; it is important that your friend never loses sight of this truth. The passages you examine after that depend on your friend's response. If your friend is puzzled about how Christ can be one with God and yet be a distinct Person, and wants to understand the nature of Christ's relationship to God as precisely as possible, then texts that systematically make the key points are best. The gospel of John contains the best passages of this type.

Although John states the basic facts clearly, he does not show how it all logically fits together. If your friend is bothered by this, simply say, "This is how God has revealed Himself in the Bible. I accept it. God is greater than my mind can fully grasp." If there is still an impasse, try to demonstrate the attractiveness of this doctrine: the wonderful light it throws on the love, power, and availability of God. Review the materials presented in chapters 10

KEY STATEMENTS REGARDING THE DEITY OF CHRIST	
John 1:1-3	Christ is God; but Christ is also a distinct person in relationship to God the Father
John 8:56-59	Christ existed eternally
John 10:30-33	There is unity between the Father and the Son
John 14:6-11	To see and know Jesus is to see and know the Father
John 20:24-29	Jesus accepted worship as God

and 11. In speaking of the Trinity, C. S. Lewis used the illustration of the sun. When you look directly at it you are blinded by its brightness, but when you look away you see that it makes all other things clear. At least three things are made clear when we accept that Jesus is one with God:

- *God comes close to us and makes Himself known to us* (John 1:14-18; 14:6-9; 17:1-3).
- *God truly loves us.* If Jesus, who died for us, is really one with God, then we are assured that God Himself loves us. Show how the emphasis of Scripture alternates between what God has done for us and what Christ has done. First the love of Christ is mentioned, then the love of God. This is one and the same love (Romans 5:6-8; 8:31-39).
- *God saves us, not anyone else.* God alone is thanked for coming to find lost sheep (Matthew 11:28-30). God alone can give rest to our souls (Luke 15:3-7).

Your friend may not ask for a systematic theological explanation of Christ's relationship to God. In this case, the need is for a practical acceptance of Jesus' lordship, along with a preliminary understanding of His status as Son of God. Chapter 17 includes several studies in the gospel of Luke that could be used. Luke

1:26-38 is helpful in seeing Jesus as Son of God. Note the mention of the Holy Spirit. It reminds us that God is spirit and that the sonship of Christ is a spiritual relationship, not a physical one. Also note Mary's attitude of submission and her affirmation that nothing is impossible with God. To show the practical implications of Jesus as Lord, look at examples of His power and authority: forgiving sins, commanding obedience, promising new life in paradise to a dying criminal, and receiving His disciples' worship.

FOR REFLECTION

1. Take some time to check your attitude toward Islam. How has your thinking changed since beginning this study?
2. Issues of debate between Muslims and Christians can quickly hurt your developing friendship and degenerate into argumentation. How can you avoid sabotaging your friendship while remaining true to your convictions and conscience?
3. Summarize the thoughts you would like to communicate to your friend about the Qur'an, the crucifixion of Jesus, the need for atonement, and the deity of Jesus. If you have trouble with any of these issues, go back and review the appropriate materials in Part 2 of this book.

CHAPTER SIXTEEN

CONTEXTUALIZATION IN AN ARAB MUSLIM ENVIRONMENT

Clear thinking about contextualization may provide significant keys for effective communication of the gospel. But contextualization, in and of itself, is not a panacea for all of the barriers faced by Muslims as they consider the good news. In order to appreciate the helpfulness of contextualization while identifying the pitfalls, there are several preliminary questions that must be addressed before practical guidelines can be recommended.

What is contextualization? The term signifies the process, or way, Christians (individually and as the church) relate to, or make use of, the sociocultural context in communicating the Christian faith and living the Christian life within their own culture. Expatriate cross-cultural workers and national Christians are involved in the process.

Is contextualization biblical? Some have charged that contextualization relativizes divine revelation and denies absolutes. The problem, however, lies not in the fact that Christians attempt to contextualize but in the way that it is done. Some approaches may undercut biblical authority, whereas others enhance biblical au-

This chapter is a distillation of material produced by the Contextualization Study Group of Arab World Ministries. This study group is engaged in ongoing research, evaluation, and strategy with reference to this subject. The material presented here comes from a preliminary report submitted in 1991.

thority. The term may be fairly new, but the phenomenon of contextualization is as old as the Bible.

Is contextualization necessary? The nature of the gospel requires contextualization. The gospel is God's message to all mankind, calling for repentance and faith, a total commitment to Christ. It necessitates the use of cultural forms that are sufficiently intelligible to arouse active faith and obedience to the gospel, but which preserve intact the original meanings our Lord intended to convey.

BASIC TERMS AND DISTINCTIONS

CULTURE AND CONTEXTUALIZATION

What is culture? In the broadest sense, it is "an integrated system of beliefs, of values, of customs, and of institutions which express these beliefs, values and customs, which binds a society together and gives it a sense of identity, dignity, security and community."[1] These different aspects of culture include *beliefs* (e.g., how people view God, reality, man's relationship to God), *values* (e.g., what people consider to be true and untrue, good and evil, moral and immoral), *customs* (e.g., how people behave, relate to others, dress, conduct business), and *institutions* (e.g., structures of government, law, religion, and commerce). One important type of custom is the system of signs or symbols that are used to communicate within the society and transmit its beliefs and values to future generations. The principal and most versatile of these is language, but other kinds of symbols are also used for purposes of communication (e.g., gestures, rituals, material objects, and architectural elements).

FORMS, MEANING, AND THE MESSAGE

All cultures use symbols for the purpose of communication. There is a distinction between the observable *form* of a symbol and the *meaning* associated with that form. For example, the Arabic word *Allah* is a linguistic form having the meaning "supreme being, God." Form and meaning are distinct, but always occur together, like the two sides of a coin. Not all forms are alike, however, and the differences between some are significant. *Allah* is a single form; but there are instances also of a *structured complex of forms,* each form with individual meaning, but together communicating a single message (e.g., *allahu akbar* is a complex form affirming that God is greater than everyone and everything). This distinction holds not just for words, but for all symbols that are used for purposes of communication. The Ritual Prayer communicates a definite message: the worshiper's submission to God in the way Muhammed prescribed, and the worshiper's solidarity with the Muslim community.

It is possible for two people to use the same form in such different ways that on a deeper level the form takes on different meanings in the two contexts. For example, consider the English term *God* and the Arabic term *Allah.* Some Christians and Muslims use the two terms interchangeably. Others hold that the two are not equivalent. Confusion arises from failing to recognize that meaning has two sides. Linguists sometimes distinguish between these two sides as *referential meaning* and *value.*[2] The terms *God* in the Bible and *Allah* in the Qur'an both have the same referential meaning. Christians and Muslims, not to mention Jehovah's Witnesses, Mormons, Hindus and others, are thus able to use the terms interchangeably without misunderstanding one another. And Arabic-speaking Christians and Muslims both use *Allah.* However, these terms have very different values in the two contexts, because the two books have very different worldviews. It does not follow, therefore, that both communities worship the one true God in truth.

TRANSLATION AND TRANSCULTURATION

Translation involves rendering the biblical text into another language; transculturation is the incarnational communication of that biblical message within the receptor culture's frame of reference. "Transculturation is to the cultural and nonverbal aspects of communication what translation is to verbal and literary forms."[3] The two are distinct but overlapping functions. Translation is necessarily restricted by the language of the biblical text; it involves some transculturation since no two languages are ever identical in structure, terminology, or usage. Transculturation is broader than translation; where the biblical text is not involved, it can be much more free in its use of local cultural forms. It includes everything involved in gospel proclamation: paraphrase, exposition, commentary, even drama and music.

Formal correspondence and *dynamic equivalence* were terms originally used to describe approaches in Bible translation. At first, the task was conceived as simply changing the language of the original, word for word, into the corresponding forms of language in the receptor audience. Distortion, misunderstanding, or incomprehension often resulted from this approach. To overcome these problems another approach, *dynamic equivalence,* was devised that allows for greater flexibility in the choice of forms used while adhering to the intended message of the original. It defines the objective in terms of an equivalence between the *response* of those to whom the Scripture was originally given and that of the receptor audience today.

AN APPROACH TO CONTEXTUALIZATION

BASIC ASSUMPTIONS

The following principles form the basis for a theological evaluation of Islam and approach to contextualization in Islamic culture.

God created the human race in His own image. He has given us the mandate of filling the earth and subduing it (Genesis 1:26-28). As God's image-bearers, all men and women possess an intuitive knowledge of God and of what He requires of them (i.e., general revelation; Psalm 19:1-4; Romans 1:19-21). Part of the uniqueness of man resides in his ability to communicate with other humans and to transmit culture from generation to generation through the use of language and other symbols. All cultures have an essentially religious nature and reflect God's image in man, albeit imperfectly. The blossoming of the various forms of cultural expression fulfills God's mandate, though it is also done very imperfectly. *Culture is a totally human phenomenon. God exists outside culture,* whereas humans are totally immersed in culture and can only communicate and understand communication in terms of the categories of culture.

Man and woman, tempted by Satan, rebelled against God. All humanity is thereby cut off from the life of God and spiritually dead (Genesis 3:17-24; Ephesians 4:17-19). All repress the knowledge of God and of His requirements, which they have received by way of general revelation; they exchange it for untruth (Romans 1:18, 22-28). As a result of this separation, repression, and Satan's influence, *human culture reflects both the image of God in man, and man's rejection of God.* Cultural activities have been corrupted and diverted from God's noble ends. No culture can claim perfection or any special status as a divine model for emulation.

God, in His providence and grace toward all people, restrains sin and corruption from bringing about humanity's total ruin and destruction (cf. Acts 17:24-27; see also Romans 2:14-15; Isaiah 44:24-25). There is no culture so alienated from God as to be totally devoid of all traces of the divine image, and no culture that cannot be transformed into a channel for communicating God's grace to mankind.

God has condescended to reveal Himself, using human culture as the medium for his self-disclosure. God set apart Abraham and his seed, the Hebrew people, transforming them into a nation to raise up to Himself a redeemed people from among all nations (Genesis 12:2-3; 1 Peter 2:9-10). He revealed Himself to mankind through the Hebrew nation, and especially in the Person and work of Jesus Christ. This self-revelation is recorded for our benefit; through prophets and apostles, He first used the Hebrew language and culture and later the Greek language and culture as mediums of revelation. Neither of these, however, have any special divine status.

The process by which God has revealed Himself to man (inspiration) is best described as a process of translation, not one of dictation. Since God transcends culture, His thoughts and His ways are incomprehensible to mankind (Isaiah 55:8-9; Romans 11:33-34). They can only be understood as they are translated in terms of human culture using human language. The written documents of the Old and New Testaments are divine truth in terms that we can understand. Under the supervision of the Holy Spirit, the prophets and apostles accurately recorded and interpreted God's dealings with His people as God's message to humankind (1 Corinthians 1:20-25; 2:6-16).

The Scriptures of the Old and New Testaments are the sole authentic repository of God's self-revelation. They bear God's authority; they are the only rule for faith and life. They alone provide the standard for determining legitimate contextualization. They are not a verbatim transcription of the speech of God in the language of heaven (as Muslims claim for the Qur'an).

The substance of the divine self-revelation is found in the gospel of the kingdom of God. God's kingdom has come in the Person and work of Jesus Christ, and it spreads through the proclamation of the forgiveness of sins and the eternal inheritance the redeemed have through Him (Mark 1:14-15; Acts 8:12; 28:31). Although revealed through culture in order that it might address humanity, the divine message transcends culture, since its source and its subject, Jesus Christ, the God-man, are from outside culture. Its very nature requires proclamation to every people and culture.

Books claiming divine authority, such as the Bible and the Qur'an, must be interpreted by the same principles and in the same manner as all other books and human communications. These principles are as native and universal to mankind as speech itself. As with all human language, the meaning of a word in a given passage is determined by the way that word is used in relation to the other words in the passage. Absoluteness cannot be claimed for any one human interpretation of Scripture. Every interpreter brings to the text a set of subjective preunderstandings, derived from personal idiosyncrasies and cultural background; these influence the understanding in profound ways. When a text is separated from the interpreter by time and culture, the meaning the author intended to convey must be distinguished from its significance for the interpreter in his or her context. The first is primary and determinative. The authority of the Bible flows from God's Holy Spirit, its divine author, who alone can interpret it authoritatively.

The translation of the Scriptures into the different languages of the world is a part of the divine plan for mankind. Translation should be carried out in accordance with sound linguistic and hermeneutical principles, taking into account both the cultural context in which they were written and that into which they are translated. An accurate translation shares in the authority of the original. Translations are set apart from all other forms of trans-culturation of the biblical message in that they are of necessity limited by the language of the text.

AN OVERVIEW

The goal of contextualization in Muslim society. Some Christians have construed contextualization to be an ill-disguised attempt to make conversion painless, to spare the convert persecution. Similarly, Muslims may view it as an attempt to present Christianity in Muslim garb, so as to deceive the masses into thinking that the contextualized Christians are essentially followers of Islam. Certainly, both of these motives are unworthy of the gospel and should never motivate our efforts. The goal of contextualization is the fulfillment of our Lord's commission as defined in Matthew 28:18-20; Luke 24:44-49; John 20:21; and Acts 1:8; that is, to present the claims of Christ clearly and persuasively, to exhort people to faith in Christ, to teach them to be His disciples, and to gather them into churches that are culturally rooted in their society of origin.

The question of contextual method. The Qur'an is probably the most powerful cultural influence in Muslim society. Therefore, every approach must make a serious effort to relate to the Qur'an and to Muslim religious thought in general. To ignore the Qur'an opens the door to all kinds of responses that are unsatisfactory. The hermeneutical method used to interpret the Bible cross-culturally serves as the key element in a contextual approach. Hermeneutics must also apply equally to other kinds of Islamic symbols that Christians might use cross-culturally. The hermeneutic determines faithfulness to Scripture. The various approaches fall naturally into two broad types or methods: synthesis and analysis.

Synthesizing approaches contextualize by starting from within Islam. They use the Qur'an in various ways as a theological starting point or source of truth, attempting to bring the Islamic and Christian perspectives closer together, in a kind of dialectical unity. Some approaches state this as a matter of principle; for others it is implicit. In either case, they tend to attribute divine authority to the Qur'an, and some actually assume it to be *a word of God.* The method is characterized by theological ambiguity and tends to undercut the authority of the Bible, distorting its message. Even with right intentions, it is possible to fall into the trap of synthesis. As outsiders to Islamic culture, we may not be aware of some of the meanings that are communicated through our use of a form. Vigilance and care are necessary.

Analytic approaches, by contrast, attempt to understand each book on its own terms. They use the Qur'an, not as a source of theological truth, but as a *cultural starting-point* for communicating biblical truth. As a matter of principle, there is no attempt to bring the Islamic and Christian perspectives closer together. The basic thrust is analysis: to understand each book first in terms of its own categories of thought in relation to the other, and then to use appropriate linguistic and cultural forms from the Qur'an and Muslim culture as vehicles for communicating the biblical message. Although respect is shown the Qur'an, there can be no ambiguity when it comes to its authority; the Bible alone is the Word of God, and care must be taken that its authority is not undercut by the use of the Qur'an. This is the only contextual method that we recommend.

CONTEXTUALIZATION AND YOUR PERSONAL LIFE

Your approach will set an example for your circle of friends. Contextualization begins with lifestyle. Consciously or unconsciously, the way you communicate the faith and live the Christian life sets an example. But as a cultural outsider, you do not have the intimate cultural knowledge that is needed to lead the way. But you cannot avoid making evaluations and choices that affect contextualization. Be aware of the influence of your choices and continually re-examine your approach to see if changes are needed.

The Muslim world is not culturally homogeneous. Muslims in Europe and North America likewise live in diverse communities. Each country, and indeed each city, is a matrix of intertwined subcultures. People may share a common language, but the differences between dialects are such as to complicate or hinder interdialect communication. Similarly, the overwhelming majority call themselves Muslim, but are not all equally devout; many are nonpracticing. You cannot therefore assume that what might be appropriate in one place or country will be appropriate elsewhere. Nor can one assume that the Christian use of a given form will be viewed everywhere the same way. The general encouragement is to develop careful observational and listening skills. Learn by watching your Muslim friends.

Lifestyle is the most subjective aspect of contextualization. Differences in personal taste and circumstance, as well as the cultural differences noted above, make it difficult to lay down universally applicable rules for the contextualization of lifestyle. Your lifestyle will depend to some extent on the person or people you are seeking to reach. There also needs to be a balance between trying to adapt your lifestyle to the culture and your freedom in Christ. Although the New Testament speaks of the need to become all things to all men (1 Corinthians 9:19-23), it also insists that the gospel makes us free (Galatians 5:1). We must not be bound either by our own culture or by that of our hearers.

SPECIFIC ASPECTS OF CULTURE

Much of what follows is written for Christians living in Arab Muslim countries. Although the specifics may be different for your situation, the general principles should be applicable. In Europe and North America, Muslim dress and custom varies widely; carefully observe your Muslim friend's behavior. Be a learner; if you ask an honest question you are likely to receive a friendly reply and explanation.

Clothing and beards. Dress codes generally reflect the Muslim values of decency, modesty, and chastity. These are Christian values as well (cf. 1 Timothy 2:9-10; 2 Peter 3:1-3), even if they are not given high priority in the West. Arab dress codes are generally more conservative than in the West, but vary considerably, even within the same city. Wearing a beard is fairly common among Arab men, but not universal. Rural areas and the older sections of cities are traditionally more conservative than the modern European sections. The clash of cultures is also evident, with Western dress and styles vying with more traditional forms. Arab culture places more importance on the way one dresses, and styles may be used to make a political or religious statement.

Dress is a particularly sensitive issue for women, in view of Islam's emphasis on modesty. In general, therefore, women in public should be careful to wear clothing that is not formfitting, that goes below the knee (even to the ankle), and covers the upper arms. A head covering may be advisable in some places. Some women have found it advisable, for their own protection, to wear a traditional woman's outer garment in public, especially in areas that tend to be traditional.

Are there limitations to the use of local dress or style of beard? In general, be wary of styles used to make a political or religious statement, such as those associated with fundamentalist Islam. For example, in Egypt the head covering worn by middle class women is associated with the Muslim Brotherhood. On university campuses in North Africa, a young woman covered from head to toe with a *Hijab* would be associated with the Muslim Sisters. Similarly, in North Africa when a man wears a white turban he is declaring that he has made the Hajj to Mecca; in the Middle East, the mustard-brown *tarbush* has the same connotation. In general, a beard is seen as a mark of maturity and dignity. Certain beard styles, however, are associated with particular groups such as the Muslim Brotherhood. Here again, observe and ask questions.

Various taboos. Muslims do not eat pork or pork products or drink wine; they consider it a sin (Qur'an 2:219; 16:115). Some Christians of Muslim background carry over these scruples into their Christian life. The biblical principle of avoiding anything that might cause offense (1 Corinthians 10:32; 2 Corinthians 6:3) should be your guide. When showing hospitality to Muslims (and to Christians of Muslim background unless they tell you otherwise) one should never serve pork, pork products, or alcoholic beverages. It is a good idea to check purchased pastries and other prepared foods to be sure that they do not contain pork products; reassure your guests that you have done so.

Muslims treat the Qur'an with utmost reverence, out of consideration that it is a heavenly book descended from God's presence; they expect Christians to treat the Bible in the same way. To avoid offense, be careful to handle the Bible respectfully. In particular, never drop it down carelessly or put it on the floor; such actions are particularly offensive.

Many of the Muslim greetings and politeness formulas may be used in social relations with Muslims (e.g., the greeting *as-salam 'alai-kum*, "Peace be upon you," and its response *wa-'alai-kum as-salam*). Muslims sometimes appear hesitant to return this greeting to strangers they know are not Muslims. Middle Eastern Christians use in its place the expression *salam bi-kum* ("Peace be with you"), or the *salam la-kum* ("Peace to you") of the Arabic Bible (cf. Romans 1:7). This, however, stems from a felt need to be different from the majority population rather than from any real difference between the two greetings. There is no religious reason not to use the Muslim greeting with Muslims. When greeting Arab Christians, however, you should respect their sensitivities.

Some common Muslim forms do conflict with Christian principles and should be avoided, e.g., the oath *wa-laah*, "by God," used by Muslims for emphasis to convince you they are telling the truth. Muslims put the *bismillah* (i.e., a shortened form for "in the name of God the Compassionate, the Merciful") at the beginning of books and repeat it when beginning practically every action, in imitation of the Qur'an. Officially, it is considered a kind of prayer to recognize God's presence or provision. You may find, however, that many Muslims think of it as a kind of magical formula for warding off evil. Some Christians have used it in their relations with Muslims, but it may send conflicting signals.

Muslim societies generally segregate the sexes socially as a way of enforcing moral behavior. If a man and woman are alone together it is automatically assumed that immorality will result. Observe local standards for relations between the sexes so that the name of Christ will not be discredited. Depending on the culture, this will include avoiding direct eye contact with members of the opposite sex (family members excluded), avoiding open show of affection toward your spouse, and modesty in the way you walk. When visiting someone, never enter a house when there is no one of your sex to invite you inside.

Hospitality is highly valued by Arabs, and an important aspect of ministry among them. Giving and receiving hospitality each have their own rules. A few basic rules: always serve guests something to drink, preferably with cake or cookies, even if the guest arrives unexpectedly; those present when mealtime comes should be invited to share the meal (the custom is for the host to insist); guests are always served lavishly, with about twice as much food as anyone can eat; tradition requires that you serve and eat with the right hand; guests may stay longer than you are accustomed to in the West; when receiving hospitality, it is important to accept something to drink, even if you sip only a token amount—refusal is tantamount to an insult.

Related to the high value placed on hospitality is the Arab attitude toward time. Arab culture is event-oriented rather than time-oriented; people, relationships, and the event are valued highly, whereas little attention is paid to punctuality. Westerners, by contrast, are strongly time-oriented. Make the effort to adapt; it may mean changing your mealtimes and the time you visit others. Be available to people and learn how to balance that out with the needs of your family.

Arab civilization has had a long and colorful cultural history, with its own unique art forms and preferred channels of communication. Learn as much as you can about the different aspects of Arab culture: its unique art forms, proverbs and parables, poetry, literature and music, history and important historical personages. Develop a sincere appreciation for the many positive aspects of Arab culture and learn how to use this knowledge to communicate the biblical message effectively. All this is an important part of the contextualization process in Arab Islamic culture.

Note that Islamic hostility toward polytheism has generally entailed the disparagement of picturing people or animals in Islamic art. This taboo does not, however, seem to be a universal or absolute prohibition, except in the case of depicting the Prophet. One finds a limited and discreet use of pictures of people and animals in some parts of the Muslim world. Muslims tend to expect Christians to have the same values in their art. Observe and ask questions. Reflect the mores of the area where you live in the way you decorate the home and communicate the gospel (e.g., flannel-graphs, books). You may find that a picture of Jesus communicates the opposite of what you want, whereas His name or a Bible verse written in beautiful Arab calligraphy can be very appealing to the Arab Muslim.

Worship forms. Islamic law prescribes five Acts of Worship (*'ibadat*) that each Muslim is obligated to perform; the preconditions and rituals required are generally quite detailed. By participating in the prescribed manner, Muslims are thought to be *actualizing* the will of God and working for eventual entry into paradise.

You should be familiar with the Acts of Worship, with their message to Muslims, and should be respectful of them. But should Christians, for example, perform the Ritual Prayer or fast the month of Ramadan in the way prescribed by Islamic law as a way of showing that Christians are people of faith? In the past, it was generally held that these forms are too closely tied to Islamic values and ideology for Christian participation. In recent years, however, some have argued that Christians *may* participate, at least in part, as a form of witness. A few are even suggesting that an Islam reinterpreted in some such way could be a kind of dynamic equivalent of Christian faith in the Muslim world. Is this approach valid?

Several issues must be considered. First, worship in Islam serves a very different function than it does in Christianity. You should analyze the meaning of the form in its Islamic context, in keeping with the analytic approach described above. Second, advocates of this attitude assume that it is possible to give these Acts of Worship a set of meanings other than what they have always had in the Muslim context. They hold that they can do so by such things as stressing that performing the rite cannot earn a person merit; in the case of ritual prayer, Qur'anic passages are replaced by chanting passages from the Bible. This is what is meant by "giving Islamic forms Christian meanings." This new approach is based on the assumption that "form may be divorced from meaning."[4]

This approach seems to be based on a simplistic view of culture and on erroneous assumptions about religious ritual.[5] It lumps all forms together and treats them as if they were all alike. Religious rituals are not just one form, as the theory assumes, but are made up of a number of forms. They are like audiovisual sentences conveying graphic and powerful messages within their respective communities. That is the reason for their existence. Islam's prayer ritual, for example, graphically portrays submission to God and solidarity with the worldwide Muslim community. The long history of use makes it impossible to separate the form from the message associated with it in the Muslim community.

We do not therefore recommend Christian participation in Islamic rituals. Their ethos is fundamentally incompatible with the biblical worldview as proclaimed in the gospel and portrayed in Christian baptism and Holy Communion. It is naive to suppose that these rituals can be performed as prescribed by Islamic law and make them mean anything other than what they have always meant to Muslims. What you may hope to convey by your participation is irrelevant. Most Muslims will understand your actions to mean either that you are a Muslim or are well on the way to becoming one.

But what about their component parts? Might some parts of the Islamic rituals be legitimately used by Christians? Or are the standing, bowing, prostration, and kneeling positions of prayer, for example, incompatible in themselves with the Christian faith? By themselves, the different positions in the prayer ritual are not necessarily Islamic and do not convey a message. The same cannot be said of the phrases and Qur'anic passages used; they are complete sentences and together their message is very definitely Islamic. These positions of prayer may all be found in the early church, as well as in ancient Israel.[6] Indeed, it has been shown that Islam actually borrowed these and other such forms from Christianity and Judaism.[7] Hence, in principle at least, it is possible that individual forms from the Ritual Prayer might legitimately be used in Christian worship.

HANDLING DISAGREEMENT

Several passages in the New Testament (Romans 14 and 1 Co-rinthians 8-10)[8] give helpful guidelines about disputed practices. These also may be applied to the handling of disagreements over contextualization. The passages distinguish two main sources of disagreement: the scruples of the convert and the associations of the practice or form. In the first instance, the form is not intrinsi-cally evil or inappropriate to the gospel in itself; it bothers the conscience of a Christian because *in his or her mind* it is associat-ed with a past way of life and religious behavior. This is the case of the so-called weak brother. In the second source of disagree-ment, the form may be neutral in itself but it has a strong *histori-cal association,* in the culture, with some evil or religious practice that is incompatible with the gospel.

FOR REFLECTION

1. Religious rituals are made up of a number of forms. They are like audiovisual sentences conveying graphic and powerful messages within their respective communities. What are the specific messages associated with each of the ritual Acts of Worship? What about Christian baptism and Holy Communion?

2. How do the following principles (from 1 Corinthians and Ro-mans) apply to the issue of contextualization?

   - Do not judge another in matters of practice when the person is bound by conscience (Romans 14:1-12).
   - Do not hinder the work of Christ, or cause another to sin against his conscience, by your exercise of Christian liberty (Romans 14:13-23; 1 Corinthians 8-10).
   - Practice forbearance and love toward one another so that all might praise God together (Romans 15:1-13).
   - Avoid forms that are associated with evil or with religious practices that are incompatible with the gospel (1 Corinthi-ans 10:1-22).
   - Consider not only whether a practice is permissible but also whether it contributes to the welfare of the church in general (1 Corinthians 10:23-33).

CHAPTER SEVENTEEN

A MODEL FOR USING THE BIBLE WITH MUSLIMS

Genuine faith results from hearing and understanding God's Word. The Holy Spirit uses the Bible to convict us of sin, righteousness, and judgment. It is possible to discuss religion with your Muslim friend without ever opening the Scripture. It is not possible, however, to adequately introduce your friend to the good news without clear and specific reference to the Bible. Ask God to convict your friend and make clear the meaning of His Word through the Holy Spirit's power. Open the Scripture. Allow your friend to observe your own spiritual thirst and God's provision for you in the Bible. Encourage your friend's exposure to the gospel by your own speech and behavior.

READ THE BIBLE

Luke's gospel is a good starting point for a Muslim just beginning to read the Bible. It begins with themes familiar to the Muslim mind: the birth of John the Baptizer, the announcement of the angel to Mary, and the unique birth of Jesus. Immediately, the Muslim is put at ease because of the familiar ground. In contrast with the gospels of Mark and John, your friend will not be faced directly with the deity of Christ; Luke does not introduce the matter in a confrontational manner until the fourth chapter. The gospel of Luke is also adapted for thematic studies that may be developed during nine sessions. If the sessions are too long, they may be further subdivided.

EVANGELISTIC STUDIES BASED ON THE GOSPEL OF LUKE AND THE PROPHECY OF ISAIAH	
Session 1 Jesus Came to Forgive Sins	
Luke 5:17-26	Jesus put spiritual needs before physical needs; He proved His authority to forgive sins
Luke 5:27-32	Jesus accepted even the worst of sinners
Luke15:1-10	God actively searches for the lost; He rejoices when a sinner repents
Luke 15:11-24	God receives sinners like a loving father
Session 2 Jesus Taught What God Requires of People	
Luke 10:25-37	Love God and your neighbor
Luke 11:37-44	Your inward attitudes are important to God
Luke 12:13-21	Life with no thought for God is dangerous
Session 3 Jesus' Death Was Not a Mistake and No Surprise to Him	
Luke 9:18-22	Jesus predicted His own death
Luke 18:31-34	The prophets predicted Jesus' death in great detail
Luke 23:26-43	Some people mistakenly identified Jesus' suffering with weakness
Luke 23:44-56	Jesus died and was buried

Session 4 Jesus Died for Our Sins (Isaiah 52:13–53:12)	
Isaiah 52:13–53:3	The prophet said that Jesus would suffer
Isaiah 53:4-6	Jesus suffered for our sins, that we might be rescued
Isaiah 53:7-9	Jesus was innocent. We deserved the punishment of death
Isaiah 53:10-12	The prophet said that Jesus would live again and justify many
Session 5 Jesus Rose from the Dead and Is Alive Today	
Luke 24:1-12	The empty tomb and the angels witness to His life
Luke 24:13-35	The living Lord fulfilled prophecy in His death and resurrection
Luke 24:36-49	Jesus can still forgive sins and bless people
Luke 24:50-53	Jesus is now in heaven
Session 6 Jesus Offers God's Blessing; Some People Reject the Offer	
Luke 7:11-17	Jesus had compassion on the needy; He had power over death
Luke 8:26-39	Jesus displayed power over Satan
Luke 14:15-34	Jesus invites people to eternal blessing; some will lose out
Luke 19:28-44	Rejection brings judgment; Jesus loves people
Session 7 People Can Come to God Through Jesus	
Luke 7:36-50	God delights in faith and gratitude

Luke 18:9-14	God rejoices to see humility and confession of sin
Luke 18:15-17	God requires empty-handed dependence
Luke 19:28-44	God expects repentance; He will give joy
Session 8 Following Jesus Includes Warnings and Promises	
Luke 12:51-53	Do not be surprised by family opposition
Luke 14:25-33	Jesus must come first; you must count the cost of following Him
Luke 8:22-25	God will be your protection in danger
Luke 12:22-31	God will provide for your needs
Session 9 Who Is Jesus? He Is Son of God and Lord	
Luke 1:26-38	His sonship is spiritual; this displays the power of God
Luke 20:9-19	Jesus is more than a prophet
Luke 10:21-24	Jesus has a unique relationship to the Father, revealing God
Luke 2:8-20	Jesus is the Lord; He possesses all power and authority

The fourth session is both preparation for and explanation of Luke's treatment of Christ's death. Since this is such a problematic issue for Muslims, it is vital to clearly establish the connection between the Prophets' declaration about Messiah's self-sacrifice and the historical record of His death in the Gospels.

A SAMPLE BIBLE READING SESSION

With the overall direction in mind, it might help to illustrate the process by examining one specific session. Two passages particularly give a good introduction to the mission of Jesus: Luke 5:17-31 and Luke 15:1-24. They are attractive texts that touch the heart while avoiding major trouble spots. They also portray conflict situations (Jesus against the Pharisees and teachers of the law) in a way that tends to put your friend immediately on Jesus' side.

JESUS CAME TO FORGIVE SINS	
Luke 5:17-26	Jesus healed the paralyzed man
Luke 5:27-31	Jesus called Levi to discipleship
Luke 15:1-7	The parable of the lost sheep
Luke 15:8-10	The parable of the lost coin
Luke 15:11-24	The parable of the lost son

This is not designed as a purely inductive study. It has a definite theme: Jesus came to forgive sins. Your role is to guide your friend's reading in a way that highlights this one topic. On the other hand, the session is not meant to be like many topical Bible studies, in the sense that you take the lead and teach. Develop an atmosphere in which the Bible *does its own talking* and your friend discovers what naturally emerges from the text. The idea is to be low-key. But at the same time you must tenaciously hold to your task of getting across the key idea.

Make use of questions prepared in advance. Have your friend read a short, natural unit of text, then begin asking questions about it. Some of these questions will require your help. Unknown terms and unfamiliar customs must be explained. But many questions ought to be labored over and answered by your friend. Don't be afraid of silence. The questions allow you to call attention to a significant point in the text. They help you evaluate whether your friend is really getting the message.

Introductory and summary statements can also be useful. Begin by saying, "You have probably noticed that Jesus did a lot of miracles and taught people about God. But the most important thing to know about Jesus, the thing that will help you understand everything else, is that Jesus came to forgive people's sins." This focuses attention right at the beginning. Remember that your goal is not to bring out every detail of the text for discussion, but to focus on details that contribute to the central topic. Try to keep things moving. Be prepared for many questions, some of them unlikely ones not on your agenda. Try to respond adequately, but avoid lengthy discussion of side issues that distract from your main point.

THE HEALING OF THE PARALYZED MAN

Read Luke 5:17-26 together with your friend. Two key ideas are contained in this text: Jesus considered forgiveness of sins even more important than the healing of a serious physical handicap, and Jesus proved He had authority to forgive sins. Ask a series of questions to focus on these points:

- *Do you know who the Pharisees and teachers of the law were?* A simple explanation is needed because these are recurring figures in the gospel. Point out that the Pharisees were very religious. They studied the Scriptures and were very strict in observing all the details of the law. They considered themselves superior to the average person. Your friend may respond with an understanding nod of the head, thinking of fundamentalist Muslims, and perhaps resenting their righteous attitude and even feeling a bit condemned by them. Your friend is in an excellent position to favor Jesus in the ensuing conflict, and perhaps even to identify with the despised sinners who appear in the next unit.
- *What was the first thing Jesus did when the paralyzed man was brought to Him for healing? Why?* This question is to force a consideration of Jesus' concern for the man's sin before a concern for his body.
- *Why did the Pharisees object to Jesus' statement that the man's sins were forgiven? Do you agree with this objection or not?* This brings out the radical nature of Jesus' state-

ment. If Jesus does not really have authority from God, His claim to forgive is blasphemy. God is the one sinned against; He is judge, and only He has the right to grant pardon. The Pharisees are correct unless Jesus can prove His authority. This passage also has significance for Christ's deity: because He is God He can forgive sins. But you need not go into these deeper implications at this point. Emphasize that Jesus is from God, empowered to forgive sins on earth.

- *How did Jesus answer the objection of the Pharisees?* Which is easier to say? Forgiveness of sins is hard to verify, but a promise of physical healing demands visible evidence. Jesus gave the evidence; in so doing He also proved that He was not lying when He claimed to forgive sins.

- *How did people react to this act of forgiving and healing?* Note the double mention of glorifying God. Your friend will probably raise a question out of simple curiosity about the title Son of Man. Answer by referring to Daniel 7:13; Jesus is the one prophesied about there. There is no need for a long explanation.

THE CALLING OF LEVI

As you read Luke 5:27-31, point out that Jesus accepted people considered by others to be the worst sinners. The proud rejected Jesus' forgiveness.

- *Do you understand who these tax collectors were?* Explain that they were collaborators with the colonial power, Rome, and corrupt cheaters of the poor. This will give your friend a sense of the utter unworthiness of these people.

- *How did Levi respond when Jesus said, "Follow me"?* Try to help your friend see how much this sign of acceptance must have meant to a man like Levi. He was willing to leave his tax-collecting, first holding a special feast in honor of Jesus.

- *What is the implication of Jesus' acceptance of Levi's invitation? What would it mean in your own culture to accept an invitation to go and eat at someone's house?* In Arab society, to accept an invitation often means that there is no barrier between you and your host, that you consider him worthy of you. To refuse an invitation implies you do not want to get involved with him, you do not trust him, and so on. So this question should help your friend appreciate the reality of a sinner's acceptance with God.

- *Why did the Pharisees object to Jesus' acceptance of the invitation? Were they right or wrong to object? Is acceptance with God possible for someone who has not done a lot of good things to earn it? What did Jesus mean by saying that a doctor helps only those who are sick? What kind of people receive Jesus' forgiveness? What kind of people do not receive it?* Questions like these are designed to lead your friend to identify with those in the "sinner" category (though you may not put it that bluntly) and to desire the acceptance that Jesus offers to the unworthy.

THE PARABLE OF THE LOST SHEEP

Luke 15:1-7 clearly shows that God rejoices when a sinner repents and turns to Him. God makes the first move toward the sinner by actively searching for those who are far away from Him. This can be a very attractive passage for a Muslim. It provides a different picture of God than the one commonly understood in Islam. Your friend will probably not have any sense that Islam is being contradicted.

- *Do you know what a parable is? What led Jesus to tell this story? What kind of person does the lost sheep resemble? Who does the shepherd resemble?* Verse 7 draws a parallel between God's rejoicing in heaven when a sinner repents and a shepherd's rejoicing when he finds his sheep. Drawing attention to this comparison can help your friend see that the parable is meant to show us something about God.

- *Did the shepherd wait at home for the sheep to return by itself? Does God wait for the sinner to come back?* With loving concern, God actively seeks people. Call attention to the phrase "he joyfully puts it on his shoulders," which gives a picture of warmth and care as well as strength.
- *How does the shepherd feel when the sheep is safely home? How does God feel when a sinner repents? How does God go after lost sheep?* The thought that God has joy over a person's repentance, that it really makes a difference to God, may come across with great impact for your friend. Point out that the mission of Jesus is God's effort to search after lost sinners. That is why Jesus spent time with sinners and tax collectors.

THE LOST COIN

Read Luke 15:8-10 with your friend. Your goal is to help your friend to see that God seeks out the sinner and rejoices when that sinner turns to Him. Each individual has definite value in God's eyes.

- *Was the coin something that the woman valued highly? Is your soul something that God values highly?* Spend some time helping your friend to consider the value of a soul before God.

THE LOST SON

In Luke 15:11-24, God receives sinners who come to Him in the same way a loving father receives his erring son.

- *What kinds of people resemble this son? Whom does the father resemble?* These questions help your friend see that the parable gives us a picture of God and sinners.
- *What does the fact that the son asked for his inheritance and left home show you about the son? Does he love his father? Is he loyal to his father?* Some have suggested that verse 12 will speak more strongly to a Middle Easterner

than to someone from Western cultural background. One idea stands out: the son despises his father, caring only for his money and wishing that the father were out of the way. Your questions can lead your friend to see how most people treat God like this, caring only for what they can get, not truly loving Him or being loyal to Him. This parable offers a somewhat different definition of "sinner." If your friend has not already begun to identify as a sinner, maybe this can provoke reaction.

- *When the son thought about going back, what was the best he expected from his father? What do people often expect from God?* The son did not understand the nature of his father's love; he expected to be treated no better than a slave. The point of these questions is to lead your friend to consider God, and how God feels about people. Make the focus personal.

- *Have you misunderstood the real heart of God? Is what you expect from God a lot less than what God really has to give? What kind of reception did the son in the story get? Did the father treat him as a slave?* The heart of the parable is seen in verses 20 and 22-24. All of the warm details of these verses should be highlighted through your questions; they should focus on the deep affection of the father for his son.

- *Do you think the son deserved this kind of reception?* Your friend is again confronted with the idea that God receives even the undeserving. The study should culminate in a reflection on the relationship of the three parables. What do they emphasize in common? How do they uniquely convey the heart of God for men?

TELL A STORY

You might introduce your friend to the gospel and the Bible by telling an interesting story. This is an effective approach because it makes use of a common Muslim practice of clothing truth in a parable or anecdote. The Bible is an obvious source of material for stories. For example, the miracles of Jesus are striking in detail and impact. They grow out of desperate human suffering and demonstrate the sufficiency of Jesus to meet the needs of people.[1] The parables of Jesus are powerful because they were spoken at critical moments when people were struggling with Christ's presentation of truth. It is likely that each parable provides the answer to a pressing question raised by Jesus' listeners. It is also possible to make use of a common story of your own invention. Some widely known folk tales may also be used to make a point. The goal is clear communication that touches the mind and heart.

Conclude the story with a well-chosen passage of Scripture to highlight the Bible's description of man's situation and need. If your friend shows any interest, try to make a definite appointment to read the Bible together. You may want to leave a copy of a Gospel and suggest a few passages to read.

FOR REFLECTION

1. What issues are repeatedly raised in the sample Bible reading session? Why are these issues so important for your Muslim friend?

2. Develop an outline and list of leading questions for another session (try session 2 or 3) similar to those provided for the sample. Do not forget to keep the major communication theme in view.

3. Examine your list of questions for the session. Do they address the major concerns or problems generally raised by Muslims? Do they take into account what you have learned about your friend?

4. Choose one interesting story, familiar through literature or folklore, to highlight a biblical truth. Consider adapting one of Jesus' parables to a contemporary situation.

CHAPTER EIGHTEEN

RESOURCES FOR MUSLIM EVANGELISM

The list of resources in this chapter may help your Muslim friend to understand the Christian message in at least two ways. First, your friend may want to personally read the books. This firsthand exposure is of special value. Second, you may want to read the book and pass along some of the information in conversation, depending on your friend's need and interest at a particular moment. Titles printed in bold typeface are especially helpful resources for you to read and use in this way. Numbers in brackets, associated with the various language editions, correspond to the number in the publishers and distributors list at the end of the chapter.

SCRIPTURE PORTIONS

Research done by the United Bible Societies indicates the value of giving Scriptures to people in several stages, according to the increasing interest and understanding of the recipients. This avoids the frequent problem of overwhelming the newly interested person with too much information. It also has the value of guided reading; you provide the portions of Scripture that will address specific needs or questions.

STAGE 1: SCRIPTURES FOR INITIAL CONTACT

These portions relate the Scriptures to the particular concerns of the recipient. These could include selections related to
health, peace, blessings, forgiveness, and justice. Allow the Scripture to be good news. Check with your local Bible Society for selections that relate to the particular concerns of your friends and
acquaintances.

STAGE 2: SCRIPTURES THAT INTRODUCE BIBLICAL CONCEPTS

For those responding to felt need selections, make use of
Scriptures that introduce biblical concepts. These portions will
move your friend from familiar and acceptable ideas to an understanding of the unique biblical concepts that are new.

- *Message of the Tawrat, Zabur and Injil*. Available from
  the United Bible Societies in English, French, and Arabic.
  This folder contains ten Scripture selections, with carefully
  selected texts from both the Old and New Testaments.
  They set forth the gospel by carefully moving from concepts Muslim people are already familiar with to concepts
  that are new. The inside cover of the folder gives the reader
  some helpful information about the Bible itself.
- The Prophets Series: *Adam, Noah, Abraham, Moses, Joseph, David, Solomon.* Available from the United Bible Societies in English. This series of seven booklets introduces
  the biblical concepts of sin, faith, redemption, and so on,
  as shown in the lives of these prophets.

STAGE 3: SCRIPTURES FOR INQUIRERS

Scriptures for inquirers include introductions and study
notes that provide background information Muslim people find
helpful.

- *The Gospel of Jesus Christ According to Luke*. This
  study edition is available through the United Bible Societ-

ies in English, Indonesian, Farsi, and Urdu. It includes an introduction, study notes, and a glossary at the back. The introduction contains information about concerns such as the original Greek texts, various translations, the inspiration of the gospel, as well as a description of the major themes of Luke's gospel. This clarifies a number of frequent misunderstandings of Muslims, clearing the way to read and understand.

- *Followers of Jesus the Messiah according to the Acts of the Apostles.* Available from the United Bible Societies in English. This study edition of Acts is a companion volume to *The Gospel of Jesus Christ* mentioned above. It provides a similar approach with study notes to that booklet. Luke and Acts work powerfully together since both were written by Luke. The first recounts the life of Jesus, and the second shows what it looks like for a group of believers to actually follow this Jesus.

If the study editions are not available in the language you need, check with a local Arab World Ministries office or the United Bible Societies to find out what is available. Bilingual Gospels may also be available. Find a way to give your friend the information included in the study edition. Also see *Holy Book of God* (listed below) as a source of information to pass on about the Scriptures.

STAGE 4: SCRIPTURES FOR NEW BELIEVERS

After reading the study editions suggested for earlier stages, your friend should be ready to read the whole New Testament and Bible. Any good study edition is appropriate at this stage. Give some consideration to matching the translation to your friend's reading ability and level of education.

LITERATURE FOR STIMULATING INTEREST

- *Words of Jesus.* Available in English [51] and Arabic [19]. This is a collection of various sayings of Jesus, along with attractive color photographs. Because there are only a few words on each page, the reader can focus more intently on those words. It makes an attractive gift, providing a good opportunity for people to taste some of Jesus' teaching and experience for themselves that the taste is good.

- *Picture Bible.* Available in English from David C. Cook in one volume; also available in French [2] and Arabic [3]. These six volumes, in cartoon format, are appreciated by both adults and children, by Christians and non-Christians. It is an enjoyable introduction to the contents of the Bible and a helpful overview of biblical history and teaching.
- *Modern Parables.* Available in Arabic [3], these brief booklets are in two series of four titles each; each booklet is about ten pages long. These are modern parables set in the Arab world and illustrate truths about Christian faith. A quality production, with large, easy-to-read script, these booklets make excellent discussion starters. An English transcript is available for the first series. The booklets were originally produced by Lilias Trotter.
- *Ultimate Questions.* Available in English [1], French [2], and Arabic [1]. These booklets are in magazine format, with attractive color photographs. They explore some of the basic questions of life and suggest Christian responses. The series is composed of several editions, including some bilingual combinations. The content varies somewhat from language to language.

BOOKLETS THAT EXPLAIN THE CHRISTIAN GOSPEL

- *What Do You Think of Christ?* Written by Abd-ul-Masih, this 30-page booklet (English, Arabic, Turkish, Urdu, Bengali) is also available on cassette (English, Arabic, Urdu) from The Good Way [10]. It provides a good introduction to Jesus. Among the major topics are these: What do you think about Christ's miraculous birth? Christ's innocence? Christ's teachings? Christ's power? Christ's sufferings? The booklet concludes with a challenge to respond to Jesus' call. The booklet and cassette work well together.

- **Beliefs and Practices of Christians**. Written by William
  Miller, long-time missionary to Iran. This 80-page book is
  available in English [6], Arabic [3], Turkish [4], Farsi [5],
  Urdu [6, 7], and Bengali [7]. It explains what Christians
  believe in a way that makes sense to Muslims. A positive
  presentation of the gospel, as well as responses to some
  common misunderstandings. Clear, relatively simple reading. A valuable resource for discussion.
- **The Way of Jesus**. By Bruce Farnham; this 255-page book
  is available in English [51] and Arabic [3]. It provides an
  excellent description of the Christian faith for the genuine
  inquirer. A serious treatment of Jesus in the Gospels, with
  particular attention to concerns of Muslim readers. It also
  explains what is involved in becoming a follower of Jesus.
  This book is a valuable resource for discussion with your
  Muslim friend.
- **People of God**. Available in English [24], French [2, 13],
  Arabic [3], Urdu [6], and Bengali, this is a correspondence
  course in four booklets, based on careful understanding of
  a Muslim worldview. It moves carefully from the Old Testament and the prophets through to the coming of Jesus. It
  can be used as a correspondence course or on a one-to-
  one basis; it is a valuable resource for discussion.
- *Where to Begin.* This is a 24-page manuscript in mimeograph format. It is available in English [29] and contains
  outlines for ten introductory Bible studies, primarily examining passages from the Gospels. These studies were developed through the author's interaction with high school
  and university students. The guides show how to help a
  student look seriously at the text of the Gospels. It also
  contains helpful suggestions about relating to Muslim
  students.
- *Islam and Christianity.* Written by B. D. Kateregga and D.
  Shenk, this 200-page book is available in English from William B. Eerdmans Publishing Co. [also 50], and French. A
  Muslim and a Christian each describe various aspects of
  their own faith and then respond to each other's descriptions. Shenk gives a clear and attractive picture of the

Christian faith. Because this book describes both Christianity and Islam, it can feel like a safe, objective place for your friend to begin an investigation of the Christian faith. The volume is also an excellent opportunity for Christians to learn about Islam from a Muslim.

- *The Torn Veil.* Written by E. Gulshan and T. Sangster; 155 pages in English [1] and French [2]. The testimony of a young Pakistani woman, a practicing Muslim from a Shi'ite family, who found life and healing in Jesus. This may be appreciated by those with varying degrees of interest in Christian faith.
- *Into the Light.* Written by S. Masood; 157 pages in English [1]. The story of the author's search for God as a boy, and later as a young man, in Pakistan's Ahmadiyya community, this book vividly portrays the difficulties of a Muslim breaking free from Islam. Helpful for those seriously considering the Christian faith.

RESOURCES TO ANSWER HARD QUESTIONS

- **Holy Book of God**. Written by David Shenk, this 69-page booklet is available in English [47] and French [2, 13]. Have Christians changed their Holy Book? The author welcomes the question, describes what the Bible is, and explains that it has not been changed. Clear and gentle. Simple but not simplistic. Give this to a friend at the same time that you give a gospel or New Testament, to give your friend some basic information about the Bible. A valuable resource for discussion.
- *Face the Facts.* By M. H. Finlay; 107 pages, available in English [1], Arabic [3], Farsi [5], and Urdu [6, 7]. This book responds to Muslim questions about the Scriptures, Jesus the Son of God, the Trinity, and others. It follows a Muslim way of thinking.
- **La Foi en Question**. Written by C. G. Moucarry, this work is available in English [51] and French [2]. Examines differences and similarities between Islam and Christianity, thus clarifying misunderstandings. The author evidences a

deep Christian commitment combined with sympathy towards Islam. Valuable resource for discussion.

- *Le Coran et La Bible à la lumière de l'histoire et de la science*. Written by William Campbell, and currently available in French [29] with English edition pending [52], this book provides a detailed response to Muslim objections about Christian faith and a consideration of the validity of Muslim beliefs and the reliability of the Qur'an. It is an important resource tool for Christians who want to understand and respond to Muslim questions and is also useful to loan to inquirers seriously dealing with these questions.

MATERIALS FOR GROWTH IN THE CHRISTIAN FAITH

- *Basic Studies in Christian Life.* Consisting of six studies in mimeograph form, and available in English [29] and Arabic [29], this work is designed for use on a weekly basis with a new believer. Each study includes daily Bible reading assignments. The course was developed in a Muslim country to fit the local context. Brief, simple, direct.
- *Survival Kit.* Written by Ralph Neighbor for the Southern Baptists and available in English, French, and Arabic [3], this is a workbook to help new believers explore the basics of their new life in Christ and to understand the practical implications of the faith.
- *Everyday Life.* Produced by Scripture Gift Mission [21] in English, French, Arabic, Farsi, and Urdu, this work gives Scripture texts providing practical guidance on the Christian life for new believers.
- *Way Ahead.* Written by N. Warren, this booklet is 15 pages in English [7] and Urdu [6, 7]. It was intended especially to help new Christians in finding the way ahead in their new life.
- *Real Life Christianity.* Written by A. Knowles and available in English [7], this work is designed especially for new Christians. It shows how to live out Christian faith in everyday life. Full of beautiful color photos. An India edition, with Third World photos, is also available.

- *Every Man a Bible Student.* Written by J. Church and available in English [1], French [2], Turkish [4], and Urdu [6], this is a collection of Scripture references on various topics. It functions as a small concordance, but organized by topic. A very practical tool for new Christians.
- **Cost of Commitment**. This book by John White is available in English [1], French [2], and Urdu [6]. It is a very positive discussion of the cost of following Jesus. We choose "to sell all to buy the pearl" because the pearl of Jesus is of such infinite value. Relevant, practical, easy to read. A valuable resource for discussion.

You should also consider using discipleship materials produced by The Navigators, Campus Crusade for Christ, InterVarsity Christian Fellowship, Neighborhood Bible Studies, and others. Be creative and adapt materials that you have found helpful; you can give clear and persuasive testimony to the way God has used them in equipping your own life.

AUDIOCASSETTES

This list includes just a few of the many cassettes available for Muslims. Since they can be easily and cheaply produced (and reproduced), a variety of audiocassettes may be available locally. Be sure to check the resources in your area.

- *Living Arabic Bible, Gospel of Luke.* Voiced in Egyptian Arabic [29] and available on three cassettes. Excellent dramatization.
- *Call of Hope Cassettes* in classical Arabic [10]. These attractive productions include music interspersed with Scripture. Individual cassettes include Mark 1-4, the Sermon on the Mount, the death and resurrection narratives, and others.
- *The Writings of Luke.* Produced by ACEB [29], these Kabyle Berber tapes of Luke and Acts are very powerful. They come in a combination package that includes six cassettes and a book. Kabyle music cassettes are also available from ACEB.

- *Permis de Sejour.* Produced by L'Ami [29] in French and North African Arabic, these materials are a creative mixture of drama, Scripture, testimony, and song.

VIDEOCASSETTES

The use of video is still relatively recent in Muslim evangelism, but a number of projects are currently underway. When ordering videocassettes, be aware of the different formats (most are VHS) and various television standards (PAL, SECAM, and NTSC); the formats and standards are not interchangeable. Special note should be taken of the *Jesus* film, available in English, Arabic [29], French [29], Kabyle [29, 35], and many other languages [34]. It portrays the life of Jesus based on Luke's gospel; a full length, professional quality production.

RESOURCE ADDRESS LISTING

The materials suggested above are available from the publishers and distributors mentioned below in this resource address listing. A number of the organizations provide quality materials in addition to the ones listed in this chapter. Since new books and materials become available regularly, it would be helpful when writing to a publisher to ask for a current catalog or publications list. For a current list of resources or questions about resource materials, you may wish also to contact Arab World Ministries at one of the following addresses:

Canada	P.O. Box 3398, Cambridge, Ontario N3H 4T3
France	B.P. 2014, 13201 Marseille, Cedex 01
Netherlands	Postbus 59292, 1040 KG Amsterdam
Great Britain	P.O. Box 51, Loughborough, Leicestershire LE11 0ZQ
United States	P.O. Box 96, Upper Darby, PA 19082-0096

In the list below the numbers in brackets correspond to the numbers mentioned in the first part of the chapter in connection with language editions of the various resources.

[1] STL Distributors
P.O. Box 48, 6 Sherman Road
Bromley, Kent BR1 3JH
United Kingdom

STL
P.O. Box 28
Waynesboro, GA 30830
USA

OM Singapore
15, Emggor Street
Reality Center No. 0503
Singapore 0207

[2] CLC "La Colline"
26160 La BEGUDE de Mazenc
France

[3] MECO Literature & Video
P.O. Box 662
Larnaca
Cyprus

[4] Orientdienst e.V.
Postfach 45 46
6200 Wiesbaden
Germany

[5] Elam Ministries
P.O. Box 1231
London W4 3RF
United Kingdom

[6] MIK
36 Ferozepur Road
Lahore 16
Pakistan

[7] Asian Books, CLC
51 The Dean
Alresford, Hants. S024 9BJ
United Kingdom

[8] Muslim Ministries/WEC
P.O. Box 1707
Fort Washington, PA 19038
USA

[9] Iranian Christians, Inc.
P.O. Box 2415
Ann Arbor, MI 48106
USA

[10] Call of Hope
D-7000 Stuttgart 10
P.O. Box 10 0827
Germany

[11] Call of Hope Malayalam
Markaz-ul-Bishara
P.O. Box 18
Manjeri 676 121
Kerala
India

[12] Henry Martin Institute
      5-8-660/1/B/1, Chirag Ali Lane
      P.O. Box 153
      Hyderabad 500001 AP
      India

[13] CPE
      P.O. Box 900
      Abijan 08
      Ivory Coast

[14] Bangladesh Baptist Press
      G.P.O. Box 78
      Cittagong
      Bangladesh

[15] Call of Hope
      Masihee Jamat
      G.P.O. Box 3507
      Dhaka
      Bangladesh

[16] Call of Hope Swahili
      Nijia ya Uzima
      P.O. Box 21012
      Nairobi
      Kenya

[17] Call of Hope Tamil
      Fellowship of Neighbors
      P.O. Box 611, Gopalapuram
      Vellore 632006
      India

[18] Call of Hope Urdu
      Nida-E-Ummeed
      P.O. Box 336
      Lucknow 226001 (U.P.)
      India

[19] Bible Society
      P.O. Box 830
      Larnaca
      Cyprus

[20] CBN
      P.O. Box 5689
      Nicosia
      Cyprus

[21] Scripture Gift Mission
      Radstock House
      3 Ecclestion Street
      London SW1 W9LZ
      United Kingdom

      Scripture Gift Mission
      P.O. Box 250
      Willow Street, PA 17584-0250
      USA

[22] Life Challenge
      P.O. Box 60875
      Nairobi
      Kenya

[23] Fellowship of Faith (FFM)
      P.O. Box 221
      746 Pape Avenue, Station J
      Toronto, Ontario M4J 4Y1
      Canada

Fellowship of Faith for Muslims
Souldern Post Office Stores
Souldern, Bicenter
Oxfordshire OX6 9JP
United Kingdom

[24] People of God
P.O. Box 16406
Nairobi
Kenya

[25] Phil Parshall
P.O. Box 2101
1299 Makati MM
Philippines

[26] Rev. Ernest Scott
P.O. Box 5602
9200 Iligan City
Philippines

[27] IBT
Box 20100
S-104 60
Stockholm
Sweden

[28] Living Bibles International,
Europe
Box 205
52400 Herrljunga
Sweden

[29] Ecole Radio Biblique
P.O. Box 2014
13201 CEDEX 01
Marseille
France

[30] Ishmaelite Salvation Association
P.O. Box 8431
St. Thomas Town
Bangalore-560-084
India

[31] ICI
Chaussee de Waterloo, 45
1640 Rhode-Saint-Genese
Brussels
Belgium

[32] ICI
P.O. Box 5749
Nicosia
Cyprus

[33] Campus Crusade
Pearl Assurance House
4 Temple Row, Birmingham
West Midlands B2 5HG
United Kingdom

[34] For the *Jesus* film only:
Campus Crusade for Christ
Arrowhead Springs
30012 Ivy Glenn Drive
Suite 200
Laguna Niguel, CA 92677
USA

Other inquiries:
Campus Crusade for Christ
100 Sunport Lane
Orlando, FL 32809
USA

[35] Campus Pour Christ
      111, Av du Dr Rosenfeld
      93230 Romainville
      France

[36] Language Recordings
      International
      6 Empress Road
      Lahore 54000
      Pakistan

[37] Arab World Ministries
      AWM Graphics
      Burfree House
      Ieville Road
      Worthing,
      West Sussex BN11 1UG
      United Kingdom

[38] International Center
      Apartado 1188
      29080 Malaga
      Spain

[39] Neighborhood Bible Studies
      Box 222
      Dobbs Ferry, NY 10522
      USA

[40] Daystar Press
      P.O. Box 1261
      Ibadan
      Nigeria

[41] Evangel Press
      P.O. Box 28963
      Nairobi
      Kenya

[42] International Missions
      P.O. Box 83070
      Mombasa, Kenya

[43] Navigators
      P.O. Box 1659
      Colorado Springs, CO 80901
      USA

[44] Abdo
      P.O. Box 561
      Larnaca
      Cyprus

[45] OM India
      Cama's, Cold Storage
      Sun Mill Compound,
      Lower Oarek
      Bombay 400 013
      India

[46] MMC
      P.O. Box 1081
      Limassol
      Cyprus

[47] Africa Christian Press
      P.O. Box 30
      Achimota
      Ghana

      Africa Christian Press
      50 Loxwood Avenue
      Worthing,
      West Sussex BN 14 7RA
      United Kingdom

[48] Gospel Recordings
     P.O. Box 62
     Gloucester GL1 5SE
     United Kingdom

[49] Jesus to Muslims
     PO Box 1804
     Benoni 1500
     Republic of South Africa

[50] Daystar University
     College Bookshop
     P.O. Box 44400
     Nairobi
     Kenya

[51] Lion Publishing plc
     Icknield Way, Tring
     Hertfordshire HP23 4LE
     United Kingdom

[52] Middle East Resources
     P.O. Box 96
     Upper Darby, PA 19082
     USA

APPENDIX 1:
ARABIC TRANSLITERATION

THE ARABIC ALPHABET AND WRITING SYSTEM			
Name of Letter	Arabic Form	Transliteration	Guide to Pronunciation
'alif	ا	aa	*f*a*d*
baa'	ب	b	*b*ig
taa'	ت	t	*t*eil
thaa'	ث	th	*th*ink
jiim	ج	j	mea*s*ure
Haa'	ح	H	no equivalent
khaa'	خ	kh	lo*ch* (Scottish)
daal	د	d	*d*ead
dhaal	ذ	dh	*th*en
raa'	ر	r	rolled *r*
zaay	ز	z	*z*oo

siin	س	s	*s*ew
shiin	ش	sh	*sh*all
Saad	ص	S	no equivalent
Daad	ض	D	no equivalent
Taa'	ط	T	no equivalent
DHaa'	ظ	DH	no equivalent
'ayn	ع	'	no equivalent
ghayn	غ	gh	no equivalent
faa'	ف	f	*f*ool
qaaf	ق	q	no equivalent
kaaf	ک	k	*k*itten
laam	ل	l	*l*ove
miim	م	m	*m*ask
nuun	ن	n	*n*ever
haa'	ه	h	*h*appy
waaw	و	w, uu	*w*eld, f*oo*d
yaa'	ي	y, ii	*y*ell, br*ee*ze
hamza	ء	'	no equivalent

APPENDIX 2:
ISLAM AND CHRISTIANITY

CONTRASTS BETWEEN ISLAM AND CHRISTIANITY		
Doctrine	**Christianity**	**Islam**
Man	Before the Fall, humanity's relationship to God was one of unbroken fellowship.	People have always been and always will be the bondslaves of God.
	Humankind fell from a spiritual state of innocence to one of guilt, condemnation, and broken fellowship with the Creator.	Humanity's Fall was physical, from a paradise in the material heavens down to this earth.
Sin	Adam's sinful nature and judgment is transmitted to all people. Jesus alone was born sinless and holy.	Our nature remains unchanged by the Fall. Every descendant of Adam is sinless at birth.

	All are constitutionally affected by sin. Human behavior gives evidence of sin's impact on every aspect of our nature and personality.	We were created weak. Our tendency to sin results from an act of God. There is no sin nature. Although this weakness is serious, it is not insurmountable.
	The Bible clearly distinguishes between sin nature, personal sin, guilt, and judgment.	Each sin is an individual act. At worst, a sin is part of a series of sinful acts.
Judgment	God is absolutely holy and righteous. All sin is condemned by His holiness and must be punished.	God guides or leads astray whomever He pleases. He is free to condemn or condone at will. Sins are classified as greater or lesser.
	Good works cannot gain God's favor, dispose Him to forgive wrong, cover sin, remove guilt and condemnation, blot out the past, or guarantee status in the future.	If God wills, good works can gain His favor, encourage forgiveness, remove guilt, etc.
Salvation	Jesus Christ alone has rendered complete obedience to God. His sinlessness enables Him to render the perfect sacrifice.	God has made humanity's burden light. We can accumulate merit and gain rewards. We can save ourselves. All we need is guidance from God to live in submission to Him.

Eternity	Heaven is a state of eternal and unbroken fellowship with God. We receive a new body, free of sin.	Paradise is the ultimate perfection of the pleasures of this world. Fellowship with God is not the ideal to be attained.

APPENDIX 3:
SCIENCE, THE BIBLE, AND THE FAITHFULNESS OF GOD

by Kurt Wood
Ph.D. in Chemistry,
University of California at Berkeley, 1981

When God led the children of Israel out of Egypt over three thousand years ago, by the hand of the prophet Moses, He gave them laws, the *Tawrat* (Torah), both to tell them how to live and to tell them the truth about Himself and the world He had made. All the nations around the children of Israel were polytheists and worshiped the sun, the moon, sea monsters, and many other idols make of wood and stone. Although today most people tend to scoff at the idea of an idol of stone or wood, during the time of Moses these idolatrous religious systems were so compelling and so rooted in people's minds that as soon as Moses' back was turned even the children of Israel—who had just been delivered by God from Pharaoh's army—made a golden idol in the shape of a calf and began to worship it.

When we begin to understand how widespread were these false ideas about God, we begin to see the importance of the teachings of the *Tawrat,* and the rest of the Bible that followed it, about the creation. God was revealing that it is *He* who created the sun, moon, and stars—they are not gods themselves. It was *God* who caused the plants to grow for food, not some fertility goddess, and it was *God* who caused the animals to grow and bear young, not some other idol in the form of a calf or bull. The power of the sea, the thunderstorms, hail, and earthquakes—all this showed *God's* power, not the power of many little deities. It is God alone who is to be worshiped.

This truth about God is not, however, acknowledged even today everywhere in the world. Most primitive cultures in the world are animist, believing in many gods. This is one of many facts that demonstrate that men suppress the truth about God and need His Word if they are to know the truth about Him. It is a sign of the love of God for all mankind that in the Bible He has made His message about the creation plain for people of every culture and epoch to understand. The children of Israel, to whom the *Tawrat* first came, were for the most part uneducated laborers. But God, who has chosen to communicate with us, has made His message plain in the Bible—it is not necessary to have a Ph.D. in astrophysics or molecular biology, or even to know how to read at all. The Bible speaks in simple terms when it talks about the creation, precisely because it is a book for all mankind.

That is why it is a mistake to expect the Bible to be a "scientific" book, in the sense that it should read like a textbook of modern chemistry or embryology. Certainly there are no contradictions between the teachings of the Bible and the facts about the universe discovered by modern science, but if the Bible were full of scientific facts only discovered in the last fifty years, how would a simple shepherd or merchant in Palestine, or a farmer in West Africa, or an Australian aborigine, understand it? When the Bible speaks about the sun, for instance, it uses language everyone can understand—"rising" and "setting," for instance—instead of talking about sunspots, and eleven-year solar cycles, and other discoveries of recent years. The Bible is, of course, a book of knowledge (*ilm*), but the knowledge about the sun that is important for everyone to know is that it is *God* who created it and who causes it to rise and set faithfully each day. Knowledge about modern science is fascinating and often useful in many areas of our lives, but it must not be confused with the really important knowledge, the kind of knowledge that leads to spiritual life, which the Bible gives us. As the *Injil* (Gospel) says, "This is eternal life, that they know You, the only true God, and Jesus Christ whom You have sent."

It is, however, no accident that modern science arose in a historical setting in which there was understanding of the Bible's teachings about creation. Science is only possible because we observe regularities in the world around us—the sun rises and sets at predictable times, heavy objects fall when we drop them, sheep give birth to baby sheep and not to rabbits. Science is the study of these regular patterns. The Bible teaches us that this regularity is a sign of the faithfulness of God—we can count on the sun rising each morning precisely because God has promised it will: "As long as the earth endures, seedtime and harvest, cold and heat, summer and winter, day and night will never cease" (Genesis 8:22). Animist cultures, which believe in many gods inhabiting sun, rocks, trees, and animals, have not developed science precisely because they have denied the existence of the faithful hand of God ordering the world around them. It is not at all surprising, then, that so many of the founders of modern science—men such as Johannes Kepler, Robert Boyle, Blaise Pascal, Isaac Newton, Michael Faraday, and James Clerk Maxwell—were devout students of the Bible.

For the believing scientist, then, the pursuit of science is an act of worship. It is bearing witness to the faithfulness of God to His promises. But even those believers who are not scientists, who have not mastered the intricacies of the atom or the circulatory system, are also able to bear witness to the faithfulness of God, because they have seen the supreme demonstration of God's faithfulness in Jesus Christ. As the Bible says, "No matter how many promises God has made, they are 'Yes' in Christ." It is through Christ that God keeps His promises of a new heart and a changed life, of righteousness, peace, and joy. We study the Bible to learn of God's faithfulness in creation, but it is our greatest joy and comfort to study it to learn the good news, given to every person on the face of the earth, of Jesus Christ.

NOTES

INTRODUCTION

1. There are a number of good English translations of the Qur'an available in addition to Pickthall. Each has a unique contribution to make in terms of literary style or literal correspondence, so you may wish to consult a variety of translations. Of special interest is the translation by Yusef Ali; the volume contains the Arabic text, original English translation, and a brief commentary along with introductory notes. Ali is widely used in North America, and is available in Great Britain.

2. *The Holy Bible, New International Version* (International Bible Society, 1973, 1978, 1984).

CHAPTER 1: FOUNDATIONAL ISSUES

1. George W. Peters, *Saturation Evangelism: Contemporary Evangelical Perspectives* (Grand Rapids: Zondervan, 1970). In particular, see chapter 25, "Biblical and Missionary Perspectives on Household Evangelism." Peters has raised important and provocative questions about the strategic importance of household evangelism in penetrating cultures with the good news. Although his focus is not exclusively on Muslim societies, the concerns he raises have direct application.

CHAPTER 2: UNDERSTANDING ISLAM

1. Christians in the region were deeply divided by a number of doctrinal controversies. In this regard, you would be helped by consulting a standard reference on church history for information on the Jacobites, Nestorians, and the dispute surrounding the use of religious icons.

2. For a listing of the suras, complete with title and the place of revelation, see *The Meaning of the Glorious Koran,* translated by Mohammed Marmaduke Pickthall (New York: Penguin, Mentor, n.d.), pp. 456-58.

3. A. Jeffery, ed., *A Reader on Islam* (The Hague, Netherlands: Mouton, 1962), p. 157.

4. Yusuf Al-Qaradawi, *The Lawful and the Prohibited in Islam,* translated by Kamal El-Helbawy, M. Moinuddin Siddiqui, and Syed Shukry (Indianapolis, Ind.: American Trust, [1960]), pp. 2, 5.

5. It would be beneficial to catalog the attributes of Allah as given in the Qur'an. These and other passages may be a helpful starting point:
   Allah the Creator: Qur'an 2:21-22; 7:54; 16:3-17
   Allah is transcendent and separate from His creation: Qur'an 59:22-24
   Allah is omnipotent: Qur'an 6:61; 13:12-13
   Allah is sovereign over all creation, including the spirit realm: Qur'an 3:26-27
   Allah is omniscient: Qur'an 6:59-60; 13:8-9
   Allah possesses many names that describe His character: Qur'an 7:180

6. The English word *genie* or *jinni* (plural, *jinn*) is strongly related to this Arabic word; in popular lore these creatures are seen as dispensing favors to quick-witted human beings. For the importance of the jinn in folk religion, see chapter 4.

7. One writer, Caesar E. Farah, has provided a summary of moral and ethical teachings from the Qur'an that he calls Islam's commandments. It is an interesting survey, but it suggests a parallel to the commandments delivered by God to Moses that is entirely foreign to the Qur'an. There is no equivalent to the Ten Commandments in Islam. See Caesar E. Farah, *Islam: Beliefs and Observances* (Woodbury, N.Y.: Barron's Educational Series, 1970), pp. 112-13.

8. A fifth book, The Scrolls of Abraham, has been lost. Muslims claim that only the Qur'an exists today exactly as it was revealed, suggesting that not a word (some say not even a syllable!) has been altered. It is further argued that in former times, human words and ideas were mixed with those of God. The Qur'an, however, records only the words of God in all of their pristine beauty.

9. Several Muslim apologists and commentators have suggested that Christ's prophesies of the coming of the Counselor (e.g., John 14:16 and other places in the Upper Room Discourse) speak clearly of Muhammed's ministry.

10. A number of suras have this as their subject. Among them: Sura 69, The Reality; Sura 75, The Rising of the Dead; Sura 82, The Cleaving; and Sura 84, The Sundering.

11. Qur'an 18:53 may refer specifically to Christians' calling upon Jesus for assistance in the day of judgment.

12. The certainty of judgment on this sin of association is described in Qur'an 4:48. Here and elsewhere, it is described as "an invention of tremendous sin."

13. The temporary nature of judgment upon Muslims is implied in places such as Qur'an 10:108. Popular traditions suggest that the fire of judgment will be a temporary place "of purgation for certain rebellious ones of the believers." See D. B. Macdonald, in H. A. Gibbs and J. H. Kramers, eds., *Shorter Encyclopedia of Islam* (Ithaca, N.Y.: Cornell U., 1957), s.v. "al-Kiyama." On the other hand, Yusef Ali seems to relate this text to the trials and tribulations in this life; see *The Holy Qur'an,* translation and commentary by Yusef Ali (N.p.: American Trust, 1977), p. 512.

14. The Qur'an is replete with descriptions of the fire of judgment and details about the blessedness that will be the reward of the faithful, if Allah wills. Much has been made of the Qur'anic descriptions of paradise. Qur'an 76:12-22 depicts it as a beautiful garden where leisure may be enjoyed and servants abound. It is a very appealing place where the labor and trouble of this life will be rewarded and forgotten. See also Qur'an 4:57.

15. Muslim theologians, like their counterparts in Christianity, have struggled to define the balance between divine sovereignty and human responsibility. In popular Islam, the events of life are often accepted with the phrase "It is written." The phrase is reminiscent of a saying attributed to Muhammed: "The first thing which God created was a pen, and He said to it, 'Write.' It said, 'What shall I write?' And God said: 'Write down the fate of every individual thing to be created.' And accordingly, the pen wrote all that was, and that will be, to eternity."

This is a clear reminder of Allah's absolute control over human history. For additional study, see Qur'an 3:145; 6:162-64; 9:50-51; 15:21-25; 25:2; 54:48-49; 87:2-3.

16. "The earliest conscious Muslim attitude on the subject seems to have been an uncompromising fatalism" (D. B. Macdonald, in Gibbs and Kramers, eds., *Shorter Encyclopedia of Islam,* s.v. "Kadar," p. 200).

17. Three set times for prayer are noted in the Qur'an (17:78-79). The established prayer times are: (1) before sunrise but when the sky is filled with light, (2) immediately after midday, (3) between three and five o'clock in the afternoon, (4) after sunset but before total darkness, and (5) at any hour of darkness.

18. Qur'an 2:184 is taken to suggest that the fast should be followed because it is proper and right, not because of pressure or obligation placed upon the Muslim by others. Yusef Ali, commenting on this text, adds: "The instincts for food, drink, and sex are strong in the animal nature, and temporary restraint from all these enables the attention to be directed to higher things."

CHAPTER 4: FOLK ISLAM

1. See Bill A. Musk, *The Unseen Face of Islam: Sharing the Gospel with Ordinary Muslims* (London: MARC, 1989), p. 124.

2. The writings of Kurt Koch and Mark Bubeck are highly recommended for their solid biblical foundation and careful balance. On the subject of demonization and believers, a helpful resource is C. Fred Dickason's *Demon Possession and the Christian* (Westchester, Ill.: Crossway, 1987). You may not agree with his conclusions, but you must consider the body of evidence he presents.

CHAPTER 5: WOMEN IN ISLAM

1. Pontificio Instituto Di Studi Arabi E D'Islamistica, *Islamic Documents*, rev. ed. (The Vatican: Pontificio Instituto Di Studi Arabi E D'Islamistica, 1987), p. 9/6.

2. For a striking portrait of traditional family life in Egypt, see Naguib Mahfouz, *Palace Walk,* trans. William Maynard Hutchins and Olive E. Kenny (New York: Doubleday, Anchor, 1990).

CHAPTER 6: ISLAM AND CHRISTIANITY

1. K. N. from Algeria; an excerpt from a letter to the Radio School of the Bible, Marseille, France.

2. A number of passages speak of Christ's return and place at the Judgment. See Qur'an 3:55; 4:159.

3. Yusef Ali, notes at Qu'ran 61:6, *The Holy Qur'an,* translation and commentary by Yusef Ali (N.p.: American Trust, 1977).

4. You must think through this issue very carefully in order to communicate clearly with Muslims. If you are struggling to understand the biblical concept of the Trinity, your own confusion on the subject will be evident. It should be remembered that the Bible maintains a perfect balance in emphasizing the unity of God, on the one hand, and the "threeness" of God on the other. See Matthew 3:16; 28:19. A helpful summary of the Christian doctrine of the Trinity, along with a brief catalog of common heretical views of that doctrine, may be found in Stuart Olyott, *The Three Are One* (Welwyn, Hertfordshire, England: Evangelical Press, 1979). The Qur'an is very clear in its denial of the Christian Trinity; see Qur'an 4:171.

5. The Qur'anic Sura 96 deals extensively with the issue of Muhammed's inspiration and the allegation that he imagined or invented the Qur'an. Muhammed's work among the Arabs is seen as parallel to the ministry of Moses among the children of Israel; the Qur'an is comparable to the *Tawrat* (Torah).

6. Qur'an 19:23-34 records that the infant Jesus spoke to members of Mary's family. See also Qur'an 2:87; 5:110.

7. At best, the Muslim sees Jesus as *a* son of Allah, similar to Adam (cf. Luke 3:38; cp. Qur'an 3:59) or Ezra (cf. Qur'an 9:30).

8. Human weakness is mentioned in Qur'an 4:28; 30:54. The Islamic view of the Fall is recorded in Qur'an 7:19-25; the passage goes on to speak of our need to submit and rectify the failure in the garden. The Fall is closely connected with the fall of Iblis, the devil; see Qur'an 7:7-18; 20:115-23; 2:36-37.

CHAPTER 7: DEVELOPING ANSWERS TO MUSLIM QUESTIONS

1. W. St. Clair Tisdall, *Christian Reply to Muslim Objections,* photo repr. ed. (Villach, Austria: Light of Life, 1980), p. 18.

2. For example, Gleason Archer, *Encyclopedia of Bible Difficulties* (Grand Rapids: Zondervan, 1982). Others are readily available.

CHAPTER 8: THE QUR'AN AND ISLAMIC TRADITION

1. For a statement of the reasons for this approach, see the beginning of the preface to W. St. Clair Tisdall, *Christian Reply to Muslim Objections,* photo repr. ed. (Villach, Austria: Light of Life, 1980), pp. 3-9.

2. Alfred Guillaume, *Islam* (Harmondsworth, Middlesex, England: Penguin, 1954), pp. 88-110.

CHAPTER 9: THE BIBLE AND MUSLIM OBJECTIONS

1. The Inspiration of the Bible is often misunderstood by Christians. Note carefully that the term refers to the product or result of the process (i.e., the writings themselves) rather than to the process itself. Common English usage tends to emphasize the latter notion, coupling it with the idea of stimulation or motivation (for example, artistic impression). Consult a standard theological reference to gain precision of thought and expression on this key doctrine.

2. Translated from *rabiTa al-'alam al-islami* (Muslim World League). February 1976, p. 40.

3. For comments on specific Arabic translations, see the Bibliography.

4. W. St. Clair Tisdall, *Christian Reply to Muslim Objections,* photo repr. ed. (Villach, Austria: Light of Life, 1980), p. 90.

5. For a lively picture of the situation, drawn from Muslim sources, see chapter 3 of Iskander Jadeed, *How Can We Share the Gospel with Our Muslim Brothers?* (Villach, Austria: Light of Life, n.d.).

6. For a helpful discussion, see C. G. Pfander, *The Balance of Truth,* rev. ed. (London, England: Religious Tract Society, 1910), part 1, chapters 2, 3, and 4.

7. The contemporary works of Ahmed Deedat and Maurice Bucaille demonstrate this trend. For a popular treatment, see Maurice Bucaille, *The Bible, The Qur'an and Science,* translated by Alastair D. Pannell and Maurice Bucaille (Indianapolis, Ind.: American Trust, 1978).

8. For more complete coverage, see William F. Campbell, *Le Coran et La Bible à la lumière de l'histoire et de la science* (The Qur'an and the Bible in the light of history and science) (Marne-la-Valée, France: Editions Farel, 1989), pp. 47-67.

9. Kurt Wood, "Science, the Bible, and the Faithfulness of God." This unpublished article is reproduced in Appendix 3.

10. I. Howard Marshall, *The Origins of New Testament Christology* (London, England: InterVarsity, 1976), p. 45.

11. From a letter sent to Radio School of the Bible. Marseille, France. [Note: "incongruity" is understood to mean internal contradiction; the passage cited is Qur'an 4:82.].

12. See Campbell, pp. 109-13. One way Muslims deal with contradictions in the Qur'an is by using the idea of abrogation, but the details and implications of this argument are rarely developed or considered.

13. For help with specific cases of apparent contradictions in the Bible, a good place to begin is the *NIV Study Bible.* It touches a large number of apparent contradictions. Beyond that, you need to engage in careful Bible study using commentaries. If you want to study the parallel passages in the Gospels on your own, get the *Synopsis of the Four Gospels,* published by the United Bible Societies. It is constructed in such a way as to permit word-for-word comparison.

14. The contents of the epistle make it clear that it was not written by Barnabas, the companion of Paul; however, it gained considerable respect among some early Christians. The epistle dates from the late first century or early second century, which puts it in an entirely different historical class from the false Gospel of

Barnabas. For more information on the Epistle of Barnabas, including a brief introduction and reliable translation, see *The Apostolic Fathers*, vol. 1, translated by Kirsopp Lake, Loeb Classical Library (London: William Heineman, 1912), pp. 337-39.

15. Lonsdale Ragg and Laura Ragg, *The Gospel of Barnabas* (Karachi, Pakistan: Begum Aisha Bawany Waqf, n.d.), pp. 2-271, passim.

16. William Campbell, *The Gospel of Barnabas: Its True Value* (Rawalpindi, Pakistan: Christian Study Centre, 1989), pp. 77-87.

17. Campbell, *Le Coran et La Bible à la lumière de l'histoire et de la science*, provides a good general discussion and a detailed, illustrated discussion of one variant reading. He also compares the history of the text of the Gospel and that of the Qur'an.

18. John Gilchrist, *The Textual History of the Qur'an and the Bible* (Villach, Austria: Light of Life, 1981), pp. 15-21.

CHAPTER 10: THE DOCTRINE OF GOD

1. Letter dated September 19, 1990, from an Algerian correspondent to Radio School of the Bible, Marseille, France.

2. Charles Hodge, *Systematic Theology*, edited by Edwin N. Gross; abridged ed. (Grand Rapids: Baker, 1988), p. 167.

3. Geoffrey W. Bromiley, in *Baker's Dictionary of Theology* (Grand Rapids: Baker, 1960), s.v. "Trinity."

CHAPTER 11: THE PERSON OF JESUS

1. W. St. Clair Tisdall, *Christian Reply to Muslim Objections*, photo repr. ed. (Villach, Austria: Light of Life, 1980), pp. 131-32.

2. H. U. Weitbrecht Stanton, *The Teaching of the Qur'an*, rev. ed. (London, England: S.P.C.K., 1969), p. 47.

3. See the chapter "A Litany of Blessings on the Prophet" in Arthur Jeffery, ed., *A Reader on Islam* (The Hague, Netherlands: Mouton, 1962), pp. 530-36, passim.

4. Muslims have a similar problem with the Bible. They think that if the Bible is the Word of God, it cannot also be the product of human thought.

5. Undated letter to Radio School of the Bible (Marseille, France) from an unidentified correspondent.

6. Iskander Jadeed, *How Can We Share the Gospel with Our Muslim Brothers?* (Villach, Austria: Light of Life, n.d.), p. 134.

7. The Church of Jesus Christ of Latter Day Saints has taught this. However, we do not accept that Mormonism is Christianity.

8. C. G. Pfander, *Balance of Truth*, rev. ed. (London: Religious Tract Society, 1910), pp. 164-65.

CHAPTER 12: THE DEATH OF JESUS

1. The Ahmadiyya sect has its own version of the story: Jesus was crucified but survived. The sect is not generally recognized as orthodox Islam. Take time to

read Iskander Jadeed's helpful booklet, *The Cross in the Gospel and the Qur'an* (Rikon, Switzerland: The Good Way, n.d.). He points to the different and conflicting views among Muslim authorities, including the view that Jesus actually died. Jadeed then turns to the Gospels to find what really happened.

2. The Arabic word translated "gathering" is *mutawffiika,* the active participle of the Arabic verb *tawaffaa,* which usually refers to death. It is rather like saying the Lord "took someone to Himself."

CHAPTER 13: A PERSPECTIVE ON MUHAMMED

1. William F. Campbell, *Le Coran et La Bible à la lumière de l'histoire et de la science* (The Qur'an and the Bible in the light of history and science) (Marne-la-Valée, France: Editions Farel, 1989), pp. 245-52. The Greek word in question can be seen in the photograph of the manuscript (p[45]) on page 248, just below a missing portion of the manuscript in the upper right quarter; this missing portion has roughly the shape of a capital "B."

2. Adapted from Dr. H. M. Clark, as found in W. St. Clair Tisdall, *Christian Reply to Muslim Objections,* photo repr. ed. (Villach, Austria: Light of Life, 1980).

CHAPTER 16: CONTEXTUALIZATION IN
AN ARAB MUSLIM ENVIRONMENT

1. *The Willowbank Report: Gospel and Culture,* Lausanne Occasional Papers, no. 2 (Wheaton, Ill.: Lausanne Committee for World Evangelization, 1978), p. 7.

2. Ferdinand de Saussure introduces this distinction in his *Course in General Linguistics,* translated by Wade Baskin (New York: McGraw-Hill, 1959), pp. 114ff. For various reasons we have preferred the term "referential meaning," borrowed from Eugene Nida, to his term "signification."

3. Daniel Shaw, "The Context of Text: Transculturation and Bible Translation," in *The Word Among Us: Contextualizing Theology for Mission Today,* edited by Dean S. Gilliland (Dallas, Tex.: Word, 1989), p. 143.

4. To date, the most important study of this subject may be Paul G. Hiebert, "Form and Meaning in the Contextualization of the Gospel," in *The Word Among Us: Contextualizing Theology for Mission Today,* pp. 101-20.

5. See Hiebert, "Form and Meaning in the Contextualization of the Gospel" in *The Word Among Us: Contextualizing Theology for Mission Today,* pp. 105-8 for an extensive critique of this assumption.

6. E.g., Standing: 1 Kings 8:22; Mark 11:25; Luke 18:11. Bowing: Genesis 24:26. Prostration (so-and-so "worshiped"): Genesis 24:26; Joshua 5:14; 2 Chronicles 20:18; Matthew 26:39. Sitting/kneeling: 1 Kings 8:54; Acts 9:40; 20:36; Ephesians 3:14.

7. J. Dudley Woodberry, "Contextualization Among Muslims: Reusing Common Pillars," in *The Word Among Us: Contextualizing Theology for Mission Today,* pp. 282-312. Particularly note pp. 285-303.

8. See Bobby Clinton, *Disputed Practices* (Coral Gables, Florida: West Indies Mission, 1975). This work is recommended for a fuller treatment of the subject.

CHAPTER 17: A MODEL FOR USING THE BIBLE WITH MUSLIMS

1. The resurrection of Lazarus (John 11) or the healing of the paralyzed man (Luke 5) can be retold with great effectiveness.

SELECTED BIBLIOGRAPHY

HISTORY, GENERAL AND CHURCH

Abun-Nasr, Jamil M. *A History of the Maghrib.* Cambridge, England: Cambridge U., 1975. The author, an associate professor in history from the University of Ibadan, writes a history of North Africa that begins with the Punic period in ancient Carthage and concludes with the independence movements of the 1950s.

Cooley, John K. *Baal, Christ, and Mohammed: Religion and Revolution in North Africa.* New York: Holt, Rinehart & Winston, 1965. In the introduction, Cooley states that his purpose is to "set out some main themes in the relationship between religious faith, alien imperialism, and the native Berber revolutionary spirit." There is a useful section on Catholic and Protestant missionary efforts of the nineteenth and twentieth centuries.

Cuoq, Joseph. *l'Eglise d'Afrique du Nord du IIe au XIIe sicle.* Paris: Editions du Centurion, 1984. A brief history of the Christian church in North Africa from its beginnings through its flourishing to its decline. Brief highlights on the contributions of Tertullian, Cyprian, and Augustine.

Gonzalez, Justo L. *A History of Christian Thought.* 3 vols. Nashville, Tenn.: Abingdon, 1970. A thoughtful and provocative treatment of the history of Christian doctrine.

Latourette, Kenneth Scott. *A History of Christianity.* New York: Harper & Row, 1953. A one-volume church history from one of the outstanding church historians of this generation.

MUHAMMED

Watt, W. Montgomery. *Muhammad: Prophet and Statesman.* Oxford, England: Oxford U., 1961. A brief account of Muhammed's life and achievements. Particularly helpful information on the social, religious, and political climate during the time of Islam's founding and early development.

Haykal, Muhammad Husayn. *The Life of Muhammad.* Translated by Ismail Ragi A. al Faruqi. Indianapolis, Ind.: North American Trust, 1976.

INTRODUCTION TO ISLAM

Ahmad, Kurshid, ed. *Islam: Its Meaning and Message.* London: The Islamic Foundation, 1980.

al Faruqi, Ismail R., and Lois Lamya al Faruqi. *The Cultural Atlas of Islam.* New York: Macmillan, 1986. The title accurately describes the diversity and wealth of this volume. Charts, maps, and other illustrations make any time spent with this volume an enriching experience. Until their tragic deaths, the al Faruqis were among the most notable Islamic scholars in North America.

Esposito, John L., ed. *Voices of Resurgent Islam.* New York: Oxford U., 1983.

Farah, Caesar E. *Islam: Beliefs and Observances.* Woodbury, N.Y.: Barron's Educational Series, 1970.

Hourani, Albert. *Arabic Thought in the Liberal Age 1798-1939.* Rev. ed. Cambridge, England: Cambridge U., 1983.

Hughes, Thomas Patrick. *Dictionary of Islam.* Safat, Kuwait: Islamic Book, 1979. Reprint of a work produced in 1885. This is a valuable, though somewhat dated, reference tool for the student of Islam.

Jeffery, Arthur. ed. *Islam: Muhammad and His Religion.* The Library of Religion, vol. 6. New York: Liberal Arts, 1958. An anthology of Islam: its doctrine, duties, and devotion.

Maududi, Abdul Sayyid A'la. *Towards Understanding Islam.* Translated by Khurshid Ahmad. Indianapolis, Ind.: Islamic Teaching Center, 1977.

FOLK RELIGION AND SPIRITUAL WARFARE

Al-Masih, Abd. *The Occult in Islam.* Villach, Austria: Light of Life, n.d.

Bubeck, Mark I. *The Adversary: The Christian Versus Demon Activity.* Chicago: Moody, 1975. Biblical insights and guidelines for those engaged in spiritual warfare.

Bubeck, Mark I. *Overcoming the Adversary.* Chicago: Moody, 1984. This practical handbook stresses the application of Christ's victory through the resource of prayer.

Musk, Bill A. *The Unseen Face of Islam: Sharing the Gospel with Ordinary Muslims.* London: MARC, 1989.

Parshall, Philip L. *Bridges to Islam: A Christian Perspective on Folk Islam.* Grand Rapids: Baker, 1983.

Stacey, Vivienne. *Christ Supreme over Satan: Spiritual Warfare, Folk Religion, and the Occult.* Lahore, Pakistan: Masihi Isha'at Khana, 1986. This practical booklet was first published in Urdu. The final chapter is a series of Bible studies to help those delivered from Satan to stand against further attacks.

CULTURAL ADJUSTMENT AND CONTEXTUALIZATION

Lingenfelter, Sherwood G., and Marvin K. Mayers. *Ministering Cross-Culturally: An Incarnational Model for Personal Relationships.* Grand Rapids: Baker, 1986. Addresses the conflict and tension that Christians from Western culture experience when they try to work with people from different cultural and social backgrounds. The authors draw heavily from the Bible for their evaluations.

Nydell, Margaret K. *Understanding Arabs: A Guide for Westerners.* Yarmouth, Maine: Intercultural, 1987. This book is filled with insights to help readers establish better relationships with Arabs.

Patai, Raphael. *The Arab Mind.* New York: Scribner, 1976. A classic analysis of Arab culture and perspective.

SOCIOLOGY, ETHNOGRAPHY

Atiya, Nayra. *Khul-Khaal: Five Egyptian Women Tell Their Stories.* Cairo, Egypt: American U. in Cairo, 1984. Engaging stories that provide a wealth of understanding for Egyptian culture.

Beck, Lois, and Nikki Keddie, eds. *Women in the Muslim World.* Cambridge, Mass.: Harvard U., 1978.

Fahmy, Mansour, ed. *La Condition de la Femme en Islam.* Paris: Al-lia, n.d.

Fernea, Elizabeth Warnock. *A Street in Marrakech.* 2d ed. Garden City, N.Y.: Doubleday, Anchor, 1975. A fascinating personal account that describes the author and her family's attempts to learn and adjust to life in Marrakech.

_____. *Guests of the Sheik: An Ethnography of an Iraqi Village.* Garden City, N.Y.: Doubleday, Anchor, 1965. The author spent the first two years of her married life in a tribal settlement on the edge of a village in southern Iraq. A well-written personal narrative.

_____, ed. *Women and the Family in the Middle East: New Voices of Change.* Austin, Tex.: U. of Texas, 1985.

Fernea, Elizabeth Warnock, and Robert A. Fernea. *The Arab World: Personal Encounters.* Garden City, N.Y.: Doubleday, Anchor, 1987. This readable account of personal meetings with people from Lebanon, Jordan, Libya, Yemen, Morocco, Egypt, Saudi Arabia, the West Bank, and Iraq includes many colorful images and lively conversations.

Hijab, Nadia. *Womanpower: The Arab Debate on Women at Work.* Cambridge, England: Cambridge U., 1988.

Mernissi, Fatima. *Beyond the Veil: Male-Female Dynamics in Modern Muslim Society.* Rev. ed. London: Al Saqi, 1985. The author, a Moroccan university professor and sociologist, examines the concepts of female sexuality in Muslim traditions.

_____. *Doing Daily Battle: Interviews with Moroccan Women.* London: Women's, 1988. This is an English translation of *Le Maroc Raconté par ses Femmes,* first published in 1984. These interviews destroy the notion that Moroccan women see themselves as helpless creatures with no possibility for change.

Rugh, Andrea B. *Family in Contemporary Egypt.* Cairo: American U. in Cairo, 1985.

CHRISTIAN THEOLOGY

Archer, Gleason L. *Encyclopedia of Bible Difficulties.* Grand Rapids: Zondervan, 1982. An admirable help: good scholarship, clearly written, presented in the order of the biblical books, and a good buy. However it is not encyclopedic in the sense that it contains the answer to every possible problem.

Berkouwer, Gerrit Cornelius. *Holy Scripture*. Studies in Dogmatics. Translated by Jack B. Rogers. Grand Rapids: Eerdmans, 1952.

Bruce, Frederic Fyvie. *The New Testament Documents*. 5th rev. ed. Downers Grove, Ill.: InterVarsity, 1966. A classic introduction to the field of textual criticism; focuses upon the reliability of the text of Scripture.

Bruce, Frederic Fyvie. *The Books and the Parchments*. Rev. ed. Westwood, N.J.: Revell, 1963. A good first book on the transcription and transmission of the Bible. Includes elementary information on how scholars have labored to determine the correct text of the Bible.

Chafer, Lewis Sperry. *Systematic Theology*. 8 vols. Dallas, Tex.: Dallas Seminary, 1947. This work has been edited by John F. Walvoord and is now available in an abridged edition (2 vols.) by Victor Books. It represents the dispensational perspective.

Erickson, Millard J. *Christian Theology*. Grand Rapids: Baker, 1986.

Finney, Charles. *Lectures on Systematic Theology*. Grand Rapids: Eerdmans, 1951. These lectures, originally delivered at Oberlin College, provide one of the clearest declarations of theology from an Arminian perspective.

Harrison, Everett F.; Geoffrey W. Bromiley; and Carl F. H. Henry. *Baker's Dictionary of Theology*. Grand Rapids: Baker, 1960.

Hodge, Charles. *Systematic Theology*. Abridged ed. Edited by Edwin N. Gross. Grand Rapids: Baker, 1988. This is a standard reference tool from the Reformed perspective.

Kenyon, Frederic. *Our Bible and the Ancient Manuscripts*. Revised by A. W. Adams. New York: Harper & Row, 1958. A worthwhile treatment of issues surrounding the writing and copying of Scripture. The majority of the book is devoted to the different approaches to determining the genuine text of Scripture from existing manuscripts. This older work has been given a renewed life and value through the able work of Adams.

Miley, John. *Systematic Theology*. 2 vols. Hendrickson, Mass.: Hendrickson, 1989. Wesleyan and Arminian tradition.

Shedd, William G. T. *Dogmatic Theology*. 3 vols. Classic Reprint Edition. Grand Rapids: Zondervan, 1969. This work was originally published in 1888.

THE QUR'AN

Asad, Muhammad. *The Message of the Qur'an.* Gibraltar: Dar Al-Andalus, 1980. This English translation with extensive notes is distributed by E. J. Brill. The notes are helpful, but sometimes modernizing (e.g., the djinn [or jinn] may be an evil influence). Asad suggests clever but not always convincing exegesis of passages that tends to affirm the authority of the Bible.

Bucaille, Maurice. *The Bible, The Qur'an and Science.* Translated by Alastair D. Pannell and Maurice Bucaille. Indianapolis, Ind.: American Trust, 1978. This work was originally published in French, May 1976, as *La Bible, le Coran et le Science,* Seghers, 3 Rue Falguire, 75725 Paris, Cedex 15, France. This book, also translated into Arabic, has been widely circulated throughout Europe and North Africa.

Commandments by God in the Qur'an. New York: Message, 1991. This is a thematic arrangement of important texts from the Qur'an, similar to *Nave's Topical Bible.* It is extremely useful for discovering the Qur'anic teaching on a particular subject or practice.

Sell, Charles Edward. *The Historical Development of the Qur'an.* 4th ed. London: Sumpkin, Marshall, 1923. This work was reprinted in 1990 by People International. Critically examines the apparent differences between suras of the Mecca and Medina periods.

The Koran Interpreted. Translated by Arthur J. Arberry. New York: MacMillan, 1955.

The Meaning of the Glorious Koran. Translated by Mohammed Marmaduke Pickthall. New York: Penguin, Mentor, n.d. This explanatory translation includes a helpful introduction and a limited index to the themes of the Qur'an. The verse numbering scheme differs from that of most other English translations, but the correct verse is usually found quite easily. Like other Muslim interpreters, Pickhall tended to avoid interpretations of the Qur'an that support Christian views.

The Holy Qur'an. Translation and commentary by A. Yusef Ali. 2d ed. N.p.: American Trust, 1977. The commentary, contained in sequentially numbered footnotes, sets this work apart. Inclusion of the Arabic text along with the English translation will be of value to many.

THE HADITH

Ahmad, Ghazi, comp. and trans. *Sayings of Muhammad.* Lahore, Pakistan: Sh. Muhammad Ashraf, 1968. A brief collection of well-known Hadiths, arranged thematically.

Al-Qaradawi, Yusuf. *The Lawful and the Prohibited in Islam.* Translated by Kamal El-Helbawy, M. Moinuddin Siddiqui, and Syed Shukry. Indianapolis, Ind.: American Trust, 1960. This volume was prepared for North American and European Muslims who often fail to maintain the practice of orthodox Islam.

Schacht, Joseph. *An Introduction to Islamic Law.* Oxford: Clarendon, 1964. Schacht provides an excellent summary of laws touching on women's rights and marital law.

THE GOSPEL OF BARNABAS

Campbell, William F. *The Gospel of Barnabas: Its True Value.* Rawalpindi, Pakistan: Christian Study Centre, 1989. This valuable booklet is available from Arab World Ministries.

Gilchrist, John. *Origins and Sources of the Gospel of Barnabas.* Christianity and Islam Series, no. 2. Durban, South Africa: Jesus to the Muslims, 1979.

Jadeed, Iskander. *The Gospel of Barnabas: A False Testimony.* Rikon, Switzerland: The Good Way, n.d. Shows that the so-called Gospel of Barnabas contradicts even the teaching of the Qur'an; therefore Muslims should stop calling it the true Gospel.

The Gospel of Barnabas. Edited and translated by Lonsdale and Laura Ragg. Karachi, Pakistan: Begum Aisha Bawany Waqf, n.d. Based on the Italian manuscript located in the Imperial Library (Vienna, Austria), this edition omits the editors' preface that was included in the Oxford edition of 1907.

ARABIC TRANSLATIONS OF THE BIBLE

Jesuit Version. This old version is preferred among Roman Catholics.

Living Arabic Bible (LAB, 1988). This is available from International Bible Society, 1820 Jet Stream Drive, Colorado Springs, CO 80921 USA. Very readable.

Sirat-ul-Masih bi-lisan 'arabi fasih (The life of the Messiah in a classical Arabic tongue) Larnaca, Cyprus: n.p., 1987. Obtainable from Sunrise Publications, P.O. Box 3021, Durham, NC 27715.

This work has stirred a bit of controversy in that it seeks to present something of a harmonization of the Gospels into Qur'anic form.

Smith-Van-Dyck Version (SVD, 1865). The standard Arabic Bible used by the Protestant churches of the Middle East; however, its language is rather difficult for Muslims.

Today's Arabic Version (TAV, scheduled for full publication in 1991). This work follows similar translational principles as those which governed *Today's English Version.* Available from the Bible Society. Very readable.

CHRISTIAN WITNESS

Burness, Margaret. *What Would You Say If . . . : Plays to help Christians Witness to Muslim women.* Ghana: Africa Christian, 1980.

———. *What Do I Say to My Muslim Friends?* London: Church Missionary Society, 1989.

Campbell, William F. *Le Coran et La Bible à la lumière de l'histoire et de la science* (The Qur'an and the Bible in the light of history and science). Marne-la-Valée, France: Editions Farel, 1989. An English edition of this book is soon to be published. This detailed work is designed to answer the questions and accusations raised by Maurice Bucaille in his book *La Bible, le Coran et la Science.* To fully appreciate this book, the reader should be familiar with Bucaille's propositions.

Challen, Ed. *To Love a Muslim!* London: Grace, 1988.

Cooper, Anne, comp. *In the Family of Abraham: Christians and Muslims Reasoning Together.* Tunbridge Wells, England: People International, 1989.

———, ed. *Ishmael My Brother: A Biblical Course on Islam.* London: Evangelical Missionary Alliance, 1985. This book, available from MARC International, provides a good overall picture of Islam and its peoples for those interested in sharing their Christian faith.

Fry, C. George, and James R. King. *Islam: A Survey of the Muslim Faith.* Grand Rapids: Baker, 1980.

Gilchrist, John. *The Textual History of the Qur'an and the Bible.* Villach, Austria: Light of Life, 1981. Replies to the Muslim apologist Ahmed Deedat, whose books, texts, and videos have spread throughout the Muslim World. The reply is directed specifically to Deedat's *Is the Bible God's Word?* Gilchrist and Deedat are based in South Africa. English and Arabic versions are available from the publisher at P.O. Box 13, 9503 Villach, Austria, or by writing to Jesus to the Muslims, P.O. Box 1804, Benoni, 1500, Republic of South Africa.

Jadeed, Iskander, *The Cross in the Gospel and the Qur'an.* Rikon, Switzerland: The Good Way, n.d. Available by writing to the publisher at P.O. Box 66, 8586 Rikon, Switzerland. This book presents a defense of Christ's death from Muslim and Christian sources.

Jadeed, Iskander. *How Can We Share the Gospel with Our Muslim Brothers?* Villach, Austria: Light of Life, n.d. A former Muslim, the author writes warmly, with exhortation. Much of the text consists of quotations from the Bible, the creeds, the Qur'an, and the great Muslim authorities. This book underscores the value of referring to sources that are important to your Muslim friend. The type is large and the English is clear, but the arrangement is not; some of the ideas are new to Western readers. Iskander Jadeed has published a number of very useful booklets in Arabic, many of which are available in English.

Jadeed, Iskander. *No! The Religion of Christ Has Not Been Abrogated.* Rikon, Switzerland: Good Way, n.d. Seeks to prove that neither the Qur'an nor the Bible supports the charge that the Qur'an abrogates the Bible. Useful.

Jones, L. Bevan. *The People of the Mosque.* 3d ed. Calcutta, India: Baptist Mission, 1959.

Nazir-Ali, Michael. *Islam: A Christian Perspective.* Exeter, England: Paternoster, 1983.

Parshall, Philip L. *The Cross and the Crescent.* Wheaton, Ill.: Tyndale, 1989.

Stacey, Vivienne. *Practical Lessons for Evangelism Among Muslims.* Wiesbaden, Germany: Orientdienst, n.d. Grows out of practical experience in work with Muslim peoples in Pakistan; emphasizes practical communication skills for making the gospel known.

Tisdall, W. St. Clair. *Christian Reply to Muslim Objections.* Photo repr. ed. Villach, Austria: Light of Life, 1980. Originally published as *A Manual of the Leading Mohammadan Objections to Christianity* (London, S.P.C.K., 1904); this volume is full of sweet wisdom and is worth having for the introduction alone. A very practical help for the traditional objections. There are a few inconveniences: an older English style, a few Latin and Greek expressions, and a different numbering of the Qur'anic verse references.

Woodberry, J. Dudley, ed. *Muslims and Christians on the Emmaus Road.* Monrovia, Calif.: MARC, 1989. Composed mainly of papers presented at a conference on Islamic-Christian themes, sponsored by the Lausanne Committee for World Evangelization, July 1987 in Zeist, Netherlands.

INDEX OF SCRIPTURES

INDEX TO THE QUR'AN

ARAB WORLD MINISTRIES: REACHING MUSLIMS TODAY

Arab World Ministries (AWM) was formed in 1881, under the name North Africa Mission (NAM). Mr. and Mrs. George Pearce, who originally went to Algeria to explore opportunities for presenting the gospel to French soldiers, found that God had other ideas. Their hearts were touched by the spiritual poverty of Muslims in North Africa. That same compassion has motivated and compelled hundreds of NAM/AWM missionaries since that date.

Reaching Muslims with the gospel has always been hard, but for about the first eighty years access to North Africa was guaranteed by the colonial powers. As independence came to North Africa, missionaries had to find a secular identity that would give them residence. Today, Christians live in the Arab world as teachers, medical personnel, engineers, and students; their common desire is to live out the good news and make Jesus known.

Personal witness is complemented by the use of media. Arab World Ministries' media work started with a radio transmitter in Morocco. It soon moved to France, and the Radio School of the Bible was founded. More recently, a well-equipped graphics unit has been established, and great advances are being made in the quality of AWM's regular printed material, so that its appearance competes favorably with literature from secular sources. The result is a professional, well-integrated ministry of radio, correspondence courses, evangelistic and discipleship literature, cassettes, and video. These materials support and enhance the ministry of workers in the Arab world.

The 1980s were years of growth and development. An outreach to Muslim Arabs living in France was consolidated. North Africa Mission changed its name to Arab World Ministries as work expanded eastward. Arab World Ministries now focuses on the whole Arab world, providing and enjoying supportive arrangements with a number of other groups.

At the beginning of the 1990s, a significant breakthrough may be in sight. Arab World Ministries is committed to place witnessing teams in one hundred strategic cities in the twenty countries of the Arab world by the year 2000. Achieving that goal will require committed prayer, considerable finance, clear strategies, and a colossal recruiting effort.

Arab World Ministries has three primary ministries:

- placing trained individuals in teams in the Arab world to engage in personal evangelism
- establishing teams in the Arab sections of European cities, where evangelism can take many forms
- continuing outreach through audio and visual media

In all these areas there are positions to fill, teams to be strengthened, tasks to be achieved, and administrative support to be provided.

Arab World Ministries believes there are signs that this is God's day for the Muslims of the Arab world. Become involved as God's instrument for reaching Muslims with the good news!

For more information about service, contact:

Arab World Ministries, U.S.A.   Arab World Ministries
P.O. Box 96   P.O. Box 3398
Upper Darby, PA 19082-0096   Cambridge, Ontario N3H 4T3
USA   Canada

Arab World Ministries
P.O. Box 51
Loughborough
Leicestershire LE11 02Q
United Kingdom

104174

Moody Press, a ministry of the Moody Bible Institute,
is designed for education, evangelization, and edification.
If we may assist you in knowing more about Christ
and the Christian life, please write us without obligation:
Moody Press, c/o MLM, Chicago, Illinois 60610.